John Lydgate (1371-1449):
A Bio-bibliography

DEREK PEARSALL

John Lydgate (1371-1449):
A Bio-bibliography

English Literary Studies
University of Victoria
1997

ENGLISH LITERARY STUDIES
Published at the University of Victoria

Founding Editor
Samuel L. Macey

ISBN 0-920604-49-8

The ELS Monograph Series is published in consultation with members of the Department by ENGLISH LITERARY STUDIES, Department of English, University of Victoria, P.O. Box 3070, Victoria, B.C., Canada, v8w 3w1.

ELS Monograph Series No. 71
© 1997 by Derek Pearsall
The cover shows a detail from the woodcut frontispiece to Lydgate's *Testament* (Richard Pynson, 1520?).

CONTENTS

ABBREVIATIONS

BL	British Library
BJRL	*Bulletin of the John Rylands Library*
BRUO	A. B. Emden, *A Biographical Register of the University of Oxford to A.D. 1500*, 3 vols. (Oxford 1957-59)
CCR	*Calendar of Close Rolls*
CFR	*Calendar of Fine Rolls*
CPR	*Calendar of Patent Rolls*
DNB	*Dictionary of National Biography*
EDR	Ely Diocesan Records
ELH	*English Literary History*
ELN	*English Language Notes*
HMSO	Her Majesty's Stationery Office
HUO	J. I. Catto and R. Evans, eds., *The History of the University of Oxford*, Vol. 2, *Late Medieval Oxford* (Oxford 1992)
IMEV	C. Brown and R. H. Robbins, *The Index of Middle English Verse* (New York 1943); and *Supplement* by R. H. Robbins and J. L. Cutler (Lexington, KY, 1965)
m.	membrane
MLN	*Modern Language Notes*
MLQ	*Modern Language Quarterly*
MP	*Minor Poems*, ed. H. N. MacCracken (see list of Modern Editions)
MWME	A. Renoir and C. D. Benson, "John Lydgate," Fasc. XVI in Vol. 6 of *A Manual of the Writings in Middle English*, ed. A. E. Hartung (New Haven 1980), pp. 1809-1920, 2071-2175

NM	*Neuphilologische Mitteilungen*
NQ	*Notes and Queries*
PMLA	*Publications of the Modern Language Association of America*
PRO	Public Record Office
UL	University Library
VCH (E)	*Victoria County History of the County of Essex,* Vol. 2 (London 1907), pp. 107-10 (the priory of Hatfield Broad Oak)
VCH (S)	*Victoria County History of the County of Suffolk,* Vol. 2 (London 1907), pp. 56-72 (the abbey of Bury St. Edmund's)

INTRODUCTION

Whatever one's view of the merits of Lydgate's poetry—there is room for a considerable difference of opinion—there is no doubt that he is the most important figure in the literary landscape of England during the first half of the fifteenth century. Acknowledged in his own life-time as the principal inheritor of the Chaucerian poetic tradition, he had enormous influence on other writers well into the sixteenth century—establishing traditions, dictating styles, and creating a vocabulary for poetry more ample and eclectic than Chaucer's. He received commissions and requests for poems from kings, dukes and earls, but also from courtly gentlemen and country gentlewomen, and from London burgesses. He fulfilled them all: he wrote more verses (something close to 140,000 lines) than any other English poet, and there are more manuscripts of his works surviving than of those of Chaucer, and far more in illustrated and de luxe copies.

The historical and documentary facts of this extraordinary career are in urgent need of reappraisal and updating. Earlier books by W. F. Schirmer and the present author were essentially "critical biographies," and devoted most of their space to assessments and appreciations of the poems. But Lydgate is probably more important for his place in the literary and political culture of his day than as a poet in the traditional literary-critical sense. This new "bio-bibliography" aims to provide the foundations for this reassessment. For the first time it provides a full account of what is known of Lydgate's life, with new material from original sources as well as fresh evaluations of known records and of the information Lydgate himself provides in his poems. There is a more rigorous analysis of what is known of his education, of his career as a paid Lancastrian propagandist, and of his relations with patrons and the literary circles of his day. One of the insights that emerges is a fresh realization of how extraordinary the career of Lydgate was, given the fact that he was a professed monk. It is, in this context, not so much that the history of fifteenth-century monasteries throws light on Lydgate's career as that the life of Lydgate necessitates a re-evaluation of fifteenth-century English monastic culture.

A complete printing of the known Lydgate life-records, all of them transcribed or re-examined from original documents in the Public Record Office, the British Library and elsewhere, enables this book to begin to do for Lydgate what the invaluable volume of *Chaucer Life-Records* by Crow and Olson has done for Chaucer studies. Previous accounts and printings of the Lydgate life-records have been selective and incomplete: only through a presentation of the records in as complete a form as is practicable can we ensure that the gaps in our knowledge are either closed or properly recognised.

The other major component of the book, in addition to the "Life" and the life-records, is bibliographical: a listing of all the manuscripts of the major works, a listing of the major manuscripts of the minor works, and a critically selective secondary bibliography paying particular attention to recent work. These materials have the advantage over other bibliographical sources of information of being up-to-date, something that is of more than usual importance, given the surge of interest in Lydgate in recent years. Lydgate studies have been lethargic in the past, but have begun to move with greater impetus, particularly as scholars of manuscript culture start to work on a range of unanswered questions in the massive Lydgate manuscript corpus, and as scholars of the "New Historicism" recognise the wealth of opportunities Lydgate offers for the exercise of their skills.

The Life of John Lydgate

The purpose of a documentary biography such as this is twofold. The first purpose is to recover as much information as is possible about the facts of Lydgate's life so that his poems can be related to the course and events of his life in terms of chronology, occasion and subject-matter. These are facts that we need to have in order to understand the poems and the ways they function. The enquiry after these facts does not take in speculation about the poet's private life or his feelings or the relation of the poems to the growth of his mind. These are speculations that might give pleasure and might even be possible with a different kind of poet, but they are irrelevant in the case of Lydgate, to whom "self-expression" would have seemed a bizarre category, at best, of poetic ambition.

The second purpose of a documentary or factual biography is to make meaningful the relation between the facts of the poet's life and the historical circumstances in which those facts are embedded and become intelligible. The argument about "social constructivism" hardly needs to be entered into: the historical circumstances of Lydgate's life are the determinants of his poetic career in the most direct way. At the same time, one must beware of allowing historically-oriented documentary biography from drifting into "His Life, His Works, His World," as if a poet's life were a brief chronicle of his time. Such an assumption would make for an interestingly capacious historical novel, but not for a soundly based understanding. "Nothing but the facts" is an impossible ambition, given the determination of facts to represent themselves in a variety of factitious and unfathomable ways, but it is the ambition here.

Thus, since there are already in existence three critical biographies of Lydgate,[1] the following brief biography is confined to the documentary records and ascertainable facts of his life, and draws upon Lydgate's poems, and the rubrics and other information pertaining to those poems in the manuscripts, only where they provide reliable, factual information. Contextual historical information, as for instance concerning monastic and court life and events, is introduced only where it has a direct bearing on the events of the poet's life.

11

In the Prologue to *The Siege of Thebes*, which was very probably completed by 1422, Lydgate portrays himself, on pilgrimage to Canterbury, meeting Chaucer's pilgrims at their inn as they prepare to set out on their return. The Host asks him who he is and where he comes from:

> I answerde my name was Lydgate,
> Monk of Bery, nygh fyfty yere of age.   (lines 92-93)

The opening eleven lines of the Prologue imitate the opening eleven lines of Chaucer's General Prologue in consisting of an astronomical periphrasis, and they refer to a rare astronomical conjunction which determines the fictional date to be 27 April 1421.[2] Lydgate chose the date as an appropriate one for the pilgrims to be setting out after an imagined three-week stay (and thirty-odd years) in Canterbury. One does not expect strict autobiographical or numerical accuracy in this sort of fictional context, but neither does one expect deliberately misleading statements, and one may deduce, therefore, that Lydgate, nearly fifty on 27 April 1421, was born in 1371. This fits well with the recorded events of his life, and with his reference to his "Mor than thre score yeeris" in the Prologue to Book VIII (line 191) of *The Fall of Princes*, very probably being written in the mid-1430s.

Lydgate was born in Lydgate (or Lidgate), as he tells us on three occasions, twice using his birth in such a humble and insignificant village as a topos of modesty and an explanation of his lack of the finer poetic skills.[3] Lydgate is a small village in Suffolk, some eight miles south-west of Bury St. Edmunds (the poet's name is still remembered there in the village church's annual fete). It was from this village that he took his surname, as was the usual practice with monks (see the list of monks' names in Appendix no. 9), when he was recruited as a boy to the neighbouring Benedictine abbey of St. Edmund's at Bury.[4] There, with intervals, he spent the remainder of his life.

Bury was one of the great Benedictine abbeys of medieval England. Founded in 1020, it had survived years of mismanagement in the fourteenth century and two assaults by the townsfolk of Bury (in 1327 and during the Peasants' Revolt in 1381), as well as the terrors of the Black Death in 1349, to enter, in the early fifteenth century, a period of comparative tranquillity. Having lost perhaps a third of its monks and monastic servants in the plague, the abbey by 1400 was back to about 60 or 80 monks, with up to 200 servants of various kinds. With vast estates in Suffolk and the surrounding counties it was one of the half-dozen richest abbeys in England, with an annual income of about £2,000. It is difficult to say what this means in modern terms, but it would be useful to think of the abbey in Lydgate's time as a powerful business corporation with assets running into many millions. The abbot was not merely the head of this wealthy corporation, but also *ex officio* a member of the upper house of Parliament. An active and energetic abbot like William Curteys (d. 1465) played a considerable part in affairs of state, and Curteys was an important source of advice and financial support for the young Henry VI in the 1440s. But most of the energies of even a powerful abbot like Curteys went into the preservation of the abbey's wealth and privileges, particularly its privilege of exemption from episcopal visitation.

At first, if he was not recruited to the abbey's song school, a boy like Lydgate went to the almonry school maintained by the abbey, and there received instruction in Latin grammar, the Scriptures and the offices of the church. It is to these years that the ageing poet ascribes the childhood and boyhood transgressions recounted in *The Testament of Dan John Lydgate* (*MP*, I.351, lines 607-69). What he says is not necessarily all untrue, but it is so formulaic and conventional and predictable a catalogue of naughtiness that, even though it may be a way of organising details of remembered individual experience, one could not use it in an account of the facts of Lydgate's life. The experience of seeing the crucifix in the cloister, with the word "Vide" written beside it (lines 740-46), when he was still not yet fifteen, is similarly part of the confessional formula according to which the *Testament* is framed.[5] But the specific biographical data that Lydgate provides are not part of a conventional formula: when he tells us that he entered the novitiate at fully fifteen years of age (line 610) and made his profession one year later (line 672), what he says can be accepted. The usual age to begin the novitiate was eighteen, and there was a rule that profession, which normally followed after a year, could not be made until nineteen, but many exceptions were allowed, and "clothing at fifteen was common in the fifteenth century."[6]

During these years Lydgate attended the monastic school, where he received more advanced instruction to prepare for ordination and possible university entrance. On 13 March 1389, according to a record which offers the first documentary evidence of his existence, he was admitted to the order of acolyte, the highest of the four minor orders preceding the major orders of subdeacon, deacon and priest, and the first for which the abbot would have to seek a bishop's authority. The bishop was Robert Braybrooke, bishop of London 1381-1404, and the ceremony took place at his church of Hadham, near Bishop's Stortford (Appendix no. 1). Bury was actually in the diocese of Norwich, but there was a long-standing feud between the abbey and the bishop of Norwich concerning episcopal visitation, and successive abbots made full use of their privilege of calling upon other bishops to admit their candidates to all orders (*ad omnes* is the abbreviated phrase in the record).[7] A few months later, on 17 December 1389, William of Cratfield, abbot of Bury 1390-1415, sent out letters dimissory for various ordinations, including that of Lydgate as subdeacon (Appendix no. 2); he is the only candidate for that order in these letters, his fellow-acolytes from 13 March, Thomas Osbern and Henry Methwold, having been ordained subdeacons on that same day. The record of Lydgate's ordination as subdeacon (Appendix no. 3) appears in the list of ordinations for 18 December 1389 in the Register of John Fordham, bishop of Ely 1388-1425, with Lydgate's first name miswritten as "Thomas" (the following name is also a Thomas). On 28 May 1393, letters dimissory went out for Lydgate's ordination as deacon (Appendix no. 4); he was ordained deacon by the bishop of Ely on 31 May (Appendix no. 5). On 4 April 1397 letters dimissory went out for his ordination as priest (Appendix no. 6), and the ordination followed on 7 April (Appendix no. 7). Lydgate's progress from acolyte to priest was comparatively slow: two of his near-contemporaries, John Tuddenham and Richard Ormysby, took four years where he took eight, and seem to represent more the norm (though they may have been older when they started).[8]

Lydgate was probably already writing poetry, though it is impossible to say what (his poetic style shows no change or development), and dangerous to assume that the undated love-poems, such as *The Complaint of the Black Knight* and *The Flower of Courtesy*, should be assigned to this early period.[9] Such poems would have been appropriate for Lydgate to write only when he had secured a measure of freedom from monastic restraint, in the 1420s. It is likely that Lydgate became acquainted with Chaucer's poetry at an early date, but extremely unlikely that he knew him personally; their paths would not have crossed. He refers frequently to Chaucer as "my maistir," and twice laments that Chaucer is no longer alive "Me to reforme, or to be my rede" (*Troy Book*, III.551), or "to amende eke and corecte / The wronge traces of my rude penne / There as I erre" (*Life of Our Lady*, II.1648-50). But he does not say that Chaucer had ever actually done this, or in more than an exemplary capacity, and elsewhere he speaks of Chaucer's generosity to fellow-poets as something he knows from hearsay ("I have herde telle," *Troy Book*, V.3524). The submission of *The Churl and the Bird* (*MP*, II.468) to the compassionate inspection of "my maistir" (lines 379-82) is not a reference to Chaucer, who is not named, but a topos of modesty derived from Lydgate's original.

Early Career, 1399-1413

The next record of Lydgate's life is of his being a student at Oxford. A letter from the Prince of Wales survives, in a miscellaneous collection of Anglo-Norman letters and petitions probably put together as a formulary, in which he makes request to the abbot and chapter of Bury that "J.L.," of whom he has heard such good reports from "R.C.," chancellor of Oxford, should be allowed to continue his studies at Oxford.[10] "R.C." is Richard Courtenay (d. 1415), who was chancellor on 24 October 1406 and probably until October 1408; re-elected 1 July 1411 but dismissed by the king in September; re-elected again on 18 November 1411, still in office 9 December 1412, out by Whitsuntide 1413, when he became bishop of Norwich.[11] Courtenay was a close friend of the prince, a chaplain of his household, and an ally in his dispute with Thomas Arundel, archbishop of Canterbury, over jurisdiction in the University of Oxford. During the last years of Henry IV's reign, the Prince of Wales (the future Henry V) was often at odds with his father, and for a period of eighteen months in 1410-11 (during his father's indisposition) he more or less ran the country in opposition to the king's policies and those of his chancellor, Arundel, his most trusted advisor.[12] Courtenay's own fragmented chancellorship reflects the prince's fortunes in this dispute. "J.L." is certainly the poet, by virtue of the prince's known interest in him and the absence in the records of other Bury monks with these initials during Courtenay's chancellorship. It is not known during which of his periods of office the letter was written, though it is usually taken to be 1406-08.

Gloucester College, where Lydgate studied, was the house for monk-students from the southern English province of the Benedictine order. It was well supported by Bury, which generally kept to the recommendation that one in twenty of the monks of a large house should attend a *studium generale*.[13] Promising students were sent there, usually in their twenties, and the majority stayed at least five years, some for many more; for a substantial number, though, "university study was a two- or three-year interlude before their return to . . . their mother houses."[14] This seems to have been the case with Lydgate, who is not recorded as having taken a degree, unlike his older and younger contemporaries William Barwe and Thomas Clare (see *BRUO*). The vague terms in which the prince refers to what Lydgate is studying (theology or canon law) may reflect simply the general terms in which Courtenay had briefed him, but may suggest too that Lydgate's program of study was not very clearly defined. It is possible to conjecture that it was this lack of clear direction in Lydgate's studies that occasioned the summons for his return to Bury and the need for the prince's intervention. The poet repaid him with faithful poetic service; but his poetry does not suggest that he ever achieved any eminence as a professional scholar, nor any depth of learning in theology.[15] His knowledge of Latin (as well as French) is good, and his reading is wide in the established authors of the medieval trivium (the curriculum for the degree of Master of Arts); but his reading is not adventurous, and, though he is a better Latinist than Chaucer, he is not so well-read.

There is an interesting reminder of Lydgate's Oxford days in Bodleian Library MS. Laud misc. 233, the verso of the end fly-leaf of which has the early fifteenth-century inscription "Iohannis Lydgate," preceded by "Sciant presentes et futuri quod ego," apparently added at a different time, though not necessarily by a different hand (see Appendix no. 30). The manuscript belonged to Bury, as is indicated in a note on the inside lining-leaf of the front cover in the hand of Henry of Kirkestede (see note 39 below), who perhaps himself obtained it from William, abbot of St. Benet of Hulme, in Norfolk, whose name appears on the page that has the Lydgate "signature." It was possibly one of the books that Lydgate took with him to Oxford. Monks commonly inscribed their names in books that they had brought from their monastery to use in their studies at Oxford.[16] Lydgate inserted his name as a mark that the book was in his possession rather than as a mark of ownership.[17] The manuscript contains Isidore's *Synonyma* and sermons by Hildebert of Le Mans, but Lydgate may characteristically have benefited from its more miscellaneous contents, such as "Versus circiter cxiv proverbiales" or "Versus lxxiv heroici proverbiales."

Gloucester College was a religious house, and the intention was to preserve the monastic atmosphere as much as possible, but the regulation of the life of the monk-student was inevitably somewhat more relaxed.[18] Prohibitions against visiting taverns and holding supper in chambers are not to be taken as indicating the norms of behaviour, but certain more modest tastes—having one's own room and books, and greater freedom to dispose one's own time and to meet and make friends—would have been implanted, and make Lydgate's subsequent career easier to understand.[19] It is not easy to say with any conviction what Lydgate was "really" like; his poetry is too conventional to allow even room for reasonable speculation. But one thing is certain about his character: he enjoyed the comforts and privileges that fame and money procured, and he put himself to considerable effort to make sure that he had them.

The Prince of Wales, who was to succeed as Henry V in 1413, may well have known Lydgate when the monk was at Oxford: there is occasional evidence of royal or aristocratic support for particular monk-students, usually with a view to employing them in the future.[20] Henry had his attention drawn to Lydgate's facility as a versifier, recognised his promise as a future Lancastrian propagandist, and perhaps saw too the possibilities for a kind of high-style religious poetry in English that would embody his own austerely orthodox piety, fulfil his desire to promote the English language as an engine of nationhood, and pre-empt the claims of the Lollards on the vernacular as a language of religion. John Shirley (d. 1456), the ubiquitous and long-lived bookman and literary factor of the first half of the fifteenth century, whose rubrics in his Lydgate manuscripts are an important source of information (and misinformation) for the dates and occasions of Lydgate's poems, reports that Lydgate wrote translations of *The Eight Verses of St. Bernard* (*MP*, I.206) for the king's use at mass, of *Benedic anima mea domino* (*MP*, I.1) in the chapel at Windsor at the request of the dean while the king was at evensong, and of *Gloriosa dicta sunt de te* (*MP*, I.315) for the bishop of Exeter. The dean is Edmund Lacy (d. 1455), bursar and master of University College 1396-99, a king's clerk from soon after 1401, dean of the chapel within the royal household 1414-17, and bishop of Exeter from 1420. He was a close friend of the prince, especially during the period of his chaplaincy to the household, when he went everywhere with him, and it is likely that they shared an interest in liturgical composition. It is possible that Lydgate spent a long time at Oxford, much longer than the periods of Courtenay's chancellorship, that he met there the prince and Lacy, and that the two together helped shape the direction and style of Lydgate's religious verse.[21]

Shirley has a rubric to Fable VII of *Isopes Fabules* saying that it was "made in Oxforde" (*MP*, II.598). It has been assumed that this means it was written, and probably the other fables too, during Lydgate's student-days—a plausible assumption, since Aesop's *Fables* was a popular Latin school text-book. Indeed, the assumption is so plausible that one suspects Shirley may have come to it unaided. This raises the whole question of his reliability as a witness.[22] He clearly knew Lydgate or at least was in close touch with him and his literary activities: he is responsible for unique copies of some fifty poems that he attributes to Lydgate, and his attributions are nearly all well supported by other external evidence and/or by strong internal evidence of style, syntax, and metre; he makes personal remarks to and about the monk in the margins of his manuscripts; he contributes many informative-sounding rubrics apparently based on intimate knowledge. When Lydgate tells us something in his poems about the events of his life or the occasions of his poems, we may assume he is telling the truth, unless he is working within some well-established biographical convention, as of the riotousness of youth or the feebleness of old age. When Shirley tells us something in his rubrics, we may assume that it is not mere carelessness or desire to deceive, though he might embroider or exaggerate for effect or in order to assist in the construction of romantic narratives of the lives of the poets,[23] or for the sake of enhancing his reputation as a communicator of inside knowledge. But he could not depart too far from the facts as they might be publicly known or readily ascertained, otherwise he would lose that very reputation. He was not writing for a distant unknown mass audience, but for a fairly small coterie of readers, and would not say things about Lydgate that they might easily know or find not to be true. On the other hand, he could embroider, within limits. So every case has to be judged on its merits: the credibility of the rubrics to the three liturgical poems is high, because of their specificity; the rubric to Fable VII is doubtful, because too easy.

Poet to Henry V, 1413-22

The Prince of Wales was already in some capacity Lydgate's patron while the monk was at Oxford. When the prince came to the throne as Henry V on 20 March 1413, it is likely that Lydgate wrote *A Defence of Holy Church* (*MP*, I.30) for him or at his request, as a recommendation of pious and orthodox behaviour and as a way of anticipating and containing the fears, of the clerical establishment especially, that the new king might be a less severe persecutor of the Lollards and less dedicated upholder of the church than Archbishop Arundel, his father's chief advisor, who resigned as chancellor on the new king's accession.[24]

But already Lydgate had been working for the prince. On Monday 31 October 1412 at 4 p. m., according to elaborate astronomical dating in the Prologue (lines 125-46), he began his vast translation of the *Historia Destructionis Troiae* of Guido della Colonna, generally called the *Troy Book*. The translation was commissioned by Henry, as Prince of Wales (Prologue, line 102), because he wished that the greatest epic story of antiquity, and the great exemplar of chivalric deeds, should be known in "oure tonge" and "y-writen as wel in oure langage / As in latyn and in frensche it is" (Prologue, lines 113-15). It was thus part of Henry's policy of encouraging the use of English, in the writing of official documents as well as in the writing of poetry, as a way of consolidating national unity and identity—in line with his larger purpose of representing himself as the symbol of that national identity.[25] Lydgate finished his translation in 1420 (V.3368) in the eighth year of Henry V (V.3373-76), that is, after 20 March 1420. He alludes (V.3399-3442) to the Treaty of Troyes, signed between England and France on 21 May 1420 (proclaimed in England 14 June 1420), and makes specific reference to the uniting of the two kingdoms after the French king's death (V.3396); there is perhaps an echo, as in *The Siege of Thebes*, of the published terms of the treaty or "conuencioun" (V.3398): "Pes & quiete, bothe nyghe and ferre, / With-oute strife, debat, or any werre" (V.3435-36). There is allusion too to the betrothal of Henry and Katherine, daughter of Charles VI, on 2 June 1420 (V.3420-26), and eager anticipation of the return to England of the royal couple (V.3429-58), which was to be on 3 February 1421. Lydgate's manner of referring to the year in which he completed the poem, "a thousand & foure hundrid yere, / And twenti ner" (V.3368-69), suggests the end of the year, that is, if computed according to the liturgical calendar, December 1420.

The Life of Our Lady was also written during the reign of Henry V, though the date of the poem is disputed.[26] A number of manuscripts, including the good early Durham manuscript (MS. Cosin V.ii.16), have colophons stating that the poem was compiled "at the excitacion and styrryng of our worshipfull prince, kyng Harry the fifthe."[27] The lack of a poetic dedication to Henry, such as Lydgate usually lavishes on a patron, suggests that the king died before the poem was "finalised" (it is not incomplete, but it could have gone on) or else that a conventional dedication to a patron was not thought appropriate in such a poem, so clearly designed for use in a monastic community or for private devotional exercises.[28] The editors of the poem point to the presentation to Henry V by Jean Galopes in 1420 of his French translation of the pseudo-Bonaventuran *Meditationes vitae Christi*, a work much used in Lydgate's *Life*, and suggest that this may have prompted Henry to encourage Lydgate in the writing of the *Life*.[29] It would be a further indication of the king's desire to encourage quasi-liturgical English composition in the high style, and of his understanding that such writing struck at the claims of the Lollards to own the religious vernacular.[30] But Henry may have had the idea of a quasi-liturgical Marian *Life* well before 1420. Internal references speak of the poem being written within one year, begun on a "long wynters nyght" and finished in the February of the following year, and the very specific allusion to the moon "ournede new" on 1 January at the beginning of Book IV has been argued by Parr to be applicable only to the years 1405, 1408 and 1416 during the relevant period.[31] Parr favours 1416, argues that the poem was composed 1415-16, and points to the special devotion shown to Our Lady in the will that Henry made before the expedition to France in 1415; one could also adduce the special threat perceived to be presented by Lollardy in that year, with Oldcastle still at large.

Lydgate was at Windsor, according to Shirley, some time between 1414 and 1417 (the years when Lacy was dean of the Royal Chapel); he was certainly in Bury for the election of the new abbot, William of Exeter, in 1415 (Appendix no. 9). At some point, he wrote the *Ballade at the Departyng of Thomas Chaucyer on Ambassade in-to France* (*MP*, II.657), which shows apparently personal knowledge of Thomas, son of Geoffrey Chaucer, of Thomas's wife ("tendre creature," line 50), of his hospitality and the reputation of his house (at Ewelme, near Oxford) as a resort of "gentilmen of heghe and lowe estate" (line 37). The only one of those gentlemen mentioned (line 43) is Sir William Moleyns (d. 1429), who was indeed Thomas's closest friend among the Oxfordshire gentry, but scholars have added (with varying degrees of plausibility), as amongst Lydgate's possible acquaintance through Thomas Chaucer, the following: Thomas Montacute, earl of Salisbury (the second husband of Thomas's daughter Alice), Richard Beauchamp, earl of Warwick (who went with Thomas on peace negotiations in 1417), William de la Pole, earl of Suffolk (Alice's third husband), John Tiptoft, earl of Worcester, and Humphrey, duke of Gloucester.[32] Thomas was an important man — sheriff of Oxfordshire, Chief Butler to the king, Speaker of the House of Commons on five occasions, member of the King's Council 1424-25 — and he knew these gentlemen well. Whether Lydgate was a visitor at Ewelme and how well he knew Thomas Chaucer and his circle are more uncertain, and one would be wary, in the absence of concrete evidence, of allocating Thomas a large role, in collaboration with Lydgate, in the formation of a new "Lancastrian poetic."[33] All the information on the matter, including the only text of the *Ballade* (BL MS. Additional 16165), comes from Shirley, who could have deduced all he tells us from the information contained in the poem itself. He adds to the *Ballade* a little poem called *My Lady Dere* (*MP*, II.420), which he calls an "amerous balade" made on the occasion of the "departyng"; it is a lover's song to his lady expressing his sorrow on leaving her and till he sees her next, and is quite appropriate to the occasion—which is perhaps what struck Shirley when he copied it in (it occurs independently in two other manuscripts). It is followed by an envoy, "Go lytel bille," addressing the lady, quite inappropriately in the context, as a disdainful mistress, and the "Devynayle par Pycard" (an anagram of the lady's name), which remains a mystery.[34] Shirley seems to be tidying his desk. As to the date of the *Ballade*, 1414, 1417 and 1420 have all been plausibly suggested:[35] Thomas was a trusted servant of the king on these often delicate diplomatic negotiations, and he was on embassy in all these years, at times for long spells. The two earlier dates seem equally acceptable, 1420 less so, since by then these absences were becoming such a regular event.

The question arises, and will arise again, as to the likelihood that Lydgate spent any length of time out of the cloister. It has become customary to assume that he did, and Knowles adds his weighty support to this view, citing the evidence of Lydgate's commissions, contacts and payments, and the more general evidence of a relaxation in the fifteenth century of the bonds of community life in the monasteries and an increase in patronal relationships between secular families and monks.[36] It is true that there were many occasions when the abbot of a house like Bury, his prior and senior obedientiaries, would have found themselves outside the cloister—at provincial chapters, parliaments, councils abroad, visitations of dependent houses, and on manorial rounds. It is true too that neglect of enclosure was one of the commonest complaints in visitation records; an important article in Henry V's program for reforming the order in 1421 was a call for a curtailment of visits in society.[37] The literary evidence, as of Chaucer's pilgrim Monk or the monk of the *Shipman's Tale*, or Lydgate's representation of himself as a pilgrim to Canterbury in the Prologue to *The Siege of Thebes*, though it may not be reliable as evidence of actual practice, suggests a degree of relaxation.

But a monk's life was generally under stringent regulation, especially in a large and comparatively well-run Benedictine house like Bury: what a monk did was always by permission of his abbot, and monks *extravagantes* were treated as apostate.[38] Henry of Kirkestede, monk of Bury (*c.* 1314-*c.* 1378), travelled all over England to compile his catalogue of ecclesiastical authors in monastic libraries,[39] but his position was quite different from that imputed to Lydgate. Though Lydgate's university career may have given him a taste for a life more outward-looking than that of the average cloistered monk, and though he may have had access to certain special freedoms in the mid- to late 1420s, we should be wary

21

of assuming too readily that he was a frequent visitor in society, especially after the election of the administratively rigorous William Curteys as abbot in 1429. As to the possibility of his personal acquaintance with members of the nobility and gentry, and others from whom he received commissions, in many cases we probably need look no further than Bury itself, which received a constant stream of visitors, including the king for a six-month stay in 1434. Many nobles and other benefactors were admitted as associates of the fraternity of the abbey, including Richard Beauchamp, earl of Warwick, and his wife Isabel, and William de la Pole, earl of Suffolk, and his wife Alice, while Thomas Beaufort, duke of Exeter, retained a lifelong attachment to the abbey and was buried there in 1427.[40] Lydgate may have visited Ewelme, but it would have been an exceptional event; to his contemporaries he was always "the monk of Bury," and Bury was where they would normally expect him to be, except during his period at Oxford and his brief priorate at Hatfield Broad Oak. His profession did not debar him from the court and city, but his presence there was always "remarkable."

Almost immediately upon completing the *Troy Book* in December 1420, Lydgate began *The Siege of Thebes*, a version of a story often associated with the siege of Troy in the medieval "Matter of Antiquity." He provides an exact astronomical date (27 April 1421) for the events of the Prologue, as we have seen in the discussion of the date of his birth, and we may assume that he was at work on the poem then, though not necessarily just beginning it. At the end of the poem, as at the end of the *Troy Book*, he seems to make specific reference to the terms of the Treaty of Troyes of May 1420 ("ut Concordia, Pax, & Tranquillitas inter praedicta Franciae & Angliae Regna perpetuo futuris temporibus observentur," etc.) in looking forward to an age of "Pees and quyet, concord and unyte" between the two realms.[41] The debate in the poem concerning the relative claims of war and peace, the declamation on the horrors of war (lines 3655-73) and the reflections on kingship and good government are more broadly relevant to English foreign policy. It is inconceivable that Henry V was not still alive (he died on 31 August 1422) when the poem was completed, since the tone of hope is unshadowed;[42] the lack of a poetic dedication is perhaps a sign that Lydgate's projected patron had died in the interim between completion and publication.

In the last months of Henry's reign, Lydgate wrote a poem *On Gloucester's Approaching Marriage* (*MP*, II.601) to Jacqueline, countess of Hainault and Holland. In his rubric to MS. Trinity R.3.20, Shirley reports that the poem was made by Lydgate "at the reuerence of my

Lady of Holand and of my Lord of Gloucestre to fore the day of theyre maryage in the desyrous tyme of theyre truwe lovyng." He does not say whether Lydgate was asked by Humphrey, duke of Gloucester, to celebrate the forthcoming marriage, or whether the poet himself was taking the initiative in trawling for new patrons.[43] It was in any case an ill-judged marriage, put together after the countess fled to England in June 1421 to escape the territorial attentions of the duke of Burgundy, and Gloucester's claim to Hainault, backed by an unsuccessful invasion in 1424, subsequently put great strain on the Anglo-Burgundian alliance which was the cornerstone of the foreign policy of John, duke of Bedford, regent in France. Lydgate's practice of accumulating conventional topics of praise and saying nothing of substance is well suited to the delicacy of the occasion, though he does speak of the marriage as bringing peace and unity between realms, citing the marriage of Katherine and Henry V (clearly still alive) as the model (lines 47-49). Jacqueline was left to Burgundy's mercies in 1424, and the marriage was annulled in 1428 so that Gloucester might marry Eleanor Cobham.[44]

Prior of Hatfield Broad Oak, 1423-30

Soon after Henry V's death, Lydgate wrote a little poem, *A Praise of Peace* (*MP*, II.785), praying, in these newly perilous days, that God may send peace between England and France. Gloucester, however, was aware of the more immediate perils of domestic faction, and it was probably he who commissioned *The Serpent of Division*, a prose history of the civil war of Caesar and Pompey designed to warn of the dangers of civil strife, the "irrecuperable harmes of division" (p. 66, lines 2-3). The text ends with the author's statement that the work was done "bi commaundemente of my moste worschipfull maistere & souereyne" (p. 66, lines 4-5) and British Library MS. Addit. 48031 (one of the two best MSS) continues with a reference to the making of "this litill translacion, the moneth of decembre the first yere of oure souvereigne lorde that now ys, King Henry the vjte." The reference to the author's "maistere & souereyne" is to the king by courtesy of Gloucester who, though not king, spoke in England with the sovereign's voice, as can be seen from the terms of reference of his appointment as protector in England, 15 December 1422, during Bedford's absence in France.[45] The work may be dated therefore to December 1422. The colophon to MS. Addit. 48031 has the attribution to Lydgate, which would be unexpected if not true, for such an un-Lydgatian work, and also the date "m*l*iiij*c*" (1400), which

23

has caused some puzzlement.[46] It is an impossible date, not least because Chaucer is spoken of in the treatise as being long dead (p. 65, line 14); also the subject of "division" is appropriate to 1422 (and is directly picked up from *Thebes*, lines 4661-88) in a way that it was not in 1400, when the theme was rebellion, not division. Some part of the correct Roman-numeral date, we may presume, was lopped off in an earlier copy of the colophon.

Meanwhile, the late king's gratitude to his faithful poetic servant was maturing posthumously. On 21 February 1423, in accordance with a promise made by the late king and by decision of the King's Council, Lydgate was granted a quarter share of the rents from a lease made to Sir Ralph Rochefort of the lands of the alien priory of Newington Longeville and of the pension of Spalding formerly appertaining to the abbey of Angers (Appendix no. 10). Newington Longeville (Oxfordshire), a cell of Longeville Giffard in Normandy, had been confiscated by the crown in 1414 in accordance with the king's new policy in relation to alien French priories and granted on a fifty-year lease to Rochefort, to whom the king owed large sums of money. Lydgate and his fellow-beneficiaries profited only briefly from the grant, for Rochefort, to whom the crown still owed money, was granted a lease for life free of rent in 1424.[47] There are no known records of any payment to Lydgate on this account.

A little later, in June 1423 according to the eighteenth-century bibliographer Tanner,[48] Lydgate was appointed prior at Hatfield Regis, or Hatfield Broad Oak, a small Benedictine priory in Essex, dedicated to the Blessed Virgin Mary and St. Melanius. Hatfield Broad Oak, a former alien priory recently expropriated and assigned as a cell to Bury, is three miles south-east of Bishop's Stortford, not very far from Bury but nearer London. There is no surviving record of his election, but it was not before 12 May 1423, when the priorate was vacant,[49] and Lydgate was certainly in office by 25 March 1425, when he is named as prior in a local charter (Appendix no. 11). It is not clear when he vacated the post. A record of 14 February 1429 refers to a plea of debt owing to one John, prior of Hatfield Regis, but it is not clear whether this is Lydgate or his successor, John Derham (sometimes called Denham).[50] John Derham or Denham was certainly prior by 1430. An eighteenth-century transcript by the Rev. W. Cole of early documents relating to Corpus Christi College, Cambridge, includes a list of early priors of Hatfield Broad Oak: one of them, John Denham, gives a discharge to the Master of the College for a sum of 11s.6d. in 8 Henry VI (1429-30).[51] In BL Additional

Charter 28614, John Denham appears as prior in a roll of escheats at court held at Hatfield in 9 Henry VI (1430-31). Edmund Canfield was elected prior on 30 April 1434, and John Derham was dead by 1435, as appears from the extract from a bull now BL Additional Charter 28612.[52]

John Lydgate was released from obedience to prior John of Hatfield on 8 April 1434 and permitted to return to his mother house at Bury "in order to lead a better life" (Appendix no. 12). He had ceased to be prior in 1429-30, and maybe earlier, and thereby had to give up the small allowance he would have received as head of the house, but had stayed on at Hatfield because the presumably more relaxed regime left him more leisure to write.[53] Hatfield was nearer to London (though still a long way from Windsor, *pace* Schirmer 1961, p. 90) and perhaps gave him also, as Green (1980, p. 190) says, "a certain freedom of movement away from the restrictions of the mother house," though absence from the cloister would still have been the exception. It seems likely that abbot Curteys would be agitating from the start of his incumbency in 1429 for the return of the abbey's distinguished son, and one suspects that the 1434 *dimissio* is a documentary record of what was already and perhaps had long been a fact.

In Paris, 1426

During the years of his priorate at Hatfield, Lydgate performed what Green (1980, p. 189) calls "a semi-official role as apologist for the Lancastrian government," and he received commissions of many other kinds from all ranks and sorts of people. He may have had official encouragement to write *The Kings of England sithen William Conqueror* (*MP*, II.710), a versified lineage of the English kings, as a means of strengthening Henry VI's title to the throne. The reference to Henry VI as "knyght" in the penultimate line of the poem may refer to the ceremony of the king's being knighted in May 1426.[54] But the decisive moment in his new career was most probably the commissioning by the earl of Warwick in 1426 of *The Title and Pedigree of Henry VI* (*MP*, II.613), a poem designed to accompany a genealogy demonstrating the claim of Henry VI to the throne of France. Lydgate, in one of his elaborate astronomical prologues (lines 290-329), tells us that it was on 28 July, when Henry VI was "of age ny fyve yer ren" (line 30), that is in 1426, that he began his translation of the French poem by Laurence Calot. Calot was a notary who served the council of the duke of Bedford, Regent in

France, and whom Bedford had engaged early in 1423 to produce a large picture and poem to be hung in Notre Dame proclaiming Henry VI's title.[55] Richard, earl of Warwick (1382-1439), was Bedford's chief captain in the field in France, junior only to Bedford's deputy, Thomas Montacute, earl of Salisbury; Lydgate may already have got to know them both, as we have seen, whether at Ewelme, Bury, or elsewhere. Warwick did not sail for France, it appears, until at the earliest July 1426,[56] and it is not clear whether he gave Lydgate the commission before he left or immediately upon his arrival in France, or whether Lydgate was himself in France to receive the commission. Shirley, of course, knows (or jumps to the conclusion) that he was: his rubric, copied in BL MS. Harley 7333, says that the poem was "made by Lydygate Iohn the monke of Bury, at Parys, by the instaunce of my Lord of Warrewyk." But the French text could have been transmitted to Lydgate in England, and it was in England of course that the English translation was wanted, to win English not French minds, and to speak to a division in England between those who wanted the expenses of the dual monarchy and Bedford's campaigns, and those who didn't.[57] *The Devowte Inuocacioun to St. Denys* (*MP* I.127), which Shirley tells us in MS. Ashmole 59 was made "at the request of Charlles the Frenshe kynge to let it beo translated oute of Frenshe in-to Englisshe," cannot be associated with Lydgate's supposed 1426 visit to France, since the only French Charles recognised as king by England during Lydgate's adult lifetime was Charles VI, who died in 1422.[58]

But the evidence of another poem, the *Danse Macabre*, would persuade one, despite the absence of external evidence in the records, that Lydgate was indeed in Paris in 1426. The poem is a close translation of a French text originally inscribed on the cloister walls of the church of the Holy Innocents in Paris in 1424-25. In the Ellesmere MS, one of the group of manuscripts which form the A-version of the poem,[59] Lydgate has an introductory "Verba translatoris" in which he warns people to remember death, "Like the exawmple whiche that at Parise / I fownde depicte ones on a walle" (lines 19-20). He tells how "frensshe clerkes" of his acquaintance urged him to translate "Owte of the frensshe Macabrees daunce" (line 24), "The whiche daunce at seint innocentis / Portreied is" (lines 35-36). At the end of the A-version there is "Lenvoye de translatoure," addressed to "my lordes and maistres" who read "this daunce" (lines 957-58): "Owte of the frensshe I drowe hit of entente . . . / And fro Paris to Inglond hit sent" (lines 665-67). He apologises for the translation:

26

> Rude of langage y was not born in fraunce
> Haue me excused my name is Jon Lidgate.   (669-70)

Unless he is simply not telling the truth, Lydgate was in Paris, presumably in 1426 to receive Warwick's commission, and saw there, on an entirely appropriate monkish outing, the newly painted Dance of Death. The absence of record of safe-conduct or payment for his trip to France is not in itself remarkable. In 1430, Lydgate received a request from John Carpenter (*c.* 1377-1442), Town Clerk of London 1417-38, to have the verses of the Danse Macabre inscribed on the cloister walls of Pardon churchyard, attached to the chapel of the Blessed Virgin Mary at St. Paul's, where Carpenter had just installed a chantry over the charnel. This became famous as "the Daunce of Poulys," as John Stow tells us in his Survey, probably deriving his information from the rubric in MS. Trinity R.3.21.[60] The B-version of the Danse may be the text provided for this second commission. (An alternative scenario would see Carpenter's as the original commission, and Lydgate in Paris in 1430 at the time of Henry's coronation there.)

While he was still in Paris in 1426, Lydgate received from the earl of Salisbury (1388-1428), Bedford's deputy in France, a further commission to translate the *Pelerinage de la vie humaine* of Guillaume de Deguileville. Salisbury we have already seen as the second husband of Alice, daughter of Thomas Chaucer, and possibly already of Lydgate's acquaintance.[61] The translator of *The Pilgrimage of the Life of Man* tells us in his Prologue that he received the commission from "my lord / Of Salysbury" (lines 122-23) in 1426 (lines 151-56), "My lord that tyme beyng at Parys" (line 157). Presumably Lydgate was still in Paris at that time, but returned to England soon after, carrying the commission with him. The absence of Lydgate's usual dedicatory epilogue suggests that the poem was completed after the death of his patron on 3 November 1428.[62] Lydgate does not name himself in the poem, and the place of the poem in the canon is dependent upon the testimony of John Stow, who names Lydgate as the author in a note in his copy of the poem in BL MS. Stowe 952 (f. 3) and also in the caption he provides for the beautiful tinted drawing that is pasted in as a frontispiece to BL MS. Harley 4826 (a manuscript containing poems by Hoccleve and Lydgate, but not the *Pilgrimage*): "Lidgate presenting his Booke, called the Pilgrime, unto the Earle of Salisbury."[63] There has been debate about the attribution, including the possibility that Lydgate may have employed help for this huge translation, completed very quickly under pressure of

27

many other commitments, but there can be no real doubt that Lydgate was commissioned to write it and had a major hand in it.[64]

Lancastrian Propagandist and Laureate Poet to Crown and Commons, 1426-32

On his return from France in late 1426 or 1427, Lydgate found himself deluged with commissions, and the next three years are the apogee of his public career as a poet. To these dates are to be ascribed the seven "Mummings" that he wrote (pageants or tableaux vivants with accompanying commentary, or mimed plays with voice-over dialogue). *The Mumming at London* (*MP*, II.682), "a desguysing to fore the gret estates of this lande, thane being at London" (MS. Trinity R.3.20), was made for an occasion during the gathering of parliament in London, almost certainly the parliament that opened on 13 October 1427.[65] It was followed in December by the *Mumming at Hertford* (*MP*, II.675), played before the king "holding his noble feest of Cristmasse in the Castel of Hertford" and "devysed by Lydegate at the request of the Countre Roullour Brys slayne at Loviers" (MS. Trinity R.3.20).[66] The only years not otherwise accounted for in the Christmas itinerary of the king and his mother are 1426 and 1427, and 1427 is to be preferred for the *Mumming at Hertford* because it is known that they were at Hertford at Easter 1428, and may be presumed to have been prolonging their stay there, as was their wont (see Green 1976). Fourteen twenty-seven also fits better with the events of Lydgate's career. Green's other reason for preferring the later date—the touch of satire he detects concerning Katherine's liaison with Owen Tudor—is not to be entertained. Katherine (1401-1437) was a wealthy woman in her own right and exerted considerable power as the king's mother and the living embodiment of his claim to the dual monarchy, and she continued to live in the royal household until 1430;[67] it is inconceivable that anyone, least of all Lydgate, would be making sly digs at her. The 1427 date is further supported by the circumstances surrounding the *Ballade on a New Year's Gift of an Eagle presented to King Henry VI* (*MP*, II.649), made by Lydgate and given to Henry and his mother, according to Shirley, "sittyng at the mete vpon the yeris day in the Castell of Hertford." The poem accompanies the New Year's gift of a signet ring with an eagle upon it, and it happens that a record survives of a warrant for payment for jewels for New Year's gifts for 12 February 1428.[68]

Shirley, from whom we get all of our information about the mummings, and all our texts of them, tells us that the *Mumming at Eltham*

(*MP*, II.672) was made by Lydgate "at Eltham in Cristmasse, for a momyng tofore the kyng and the Qwene" (MS. Trinity R.3.20). The king and his mother were at Eltham for Christmas in 1425 and 1428: either date is possible for Lydgate's poem, though the latter much more likely, given the scenario for his activities sketched out here. He was soon in action again, for Shirley records that the *Mumming for the Mercers of London* (*MP*, II.695) was done "to fore the Mayre of London, Eestfield, vpon the twelffethe night of Cristmasse, ordeyned ryallych by the worthy merciers" (MS. Trinity R.3.20). William Eastfield was twice Mayor, in 1429 and 1437, and it is clearly to his first year of office that Shirley must allude. Mayors of London took office at Michaelmas but their year of office was counted as the calendar year following, so the *Mumming for the Mercers* was performed on 6 January 1429. Less than a month later, the *Mumming for the Goldsmiths of London* (*MP*, I.698) was mummed by the goldsmiths "to theyre Mayre Eestfeld, vpon Candelmasse day at nyght, affter souper" (MS. Trinity R.3.20), that is, on 2 February 1429. At some time during this period of London activity, and most probably in this *annus mirabilis* of 1429, the *Mumming at Bishopswood* (*MP*, II.668) was made by Lydgate and "sente by a poursyvant to the Shirreves of London, acompanyed with theire bretherne vpon Mayes daye at Busshopes wod, at an honurable dyner, eche of hem bringginge his dysshe" (MS. Ashmole 59).

Later in 1429 Lydgate wrote the *Mumming at Windsor* (*MP*, II.691) for performance before the king, "being in his Castell of Wyndesore, the fest of his Crystmasse holding ther" (MS. Trinity R.3.20). The mumming refers to the custom established by Clovis of having French kings crowned at Reims—a custom which Henry VI is about to follow. Charles VII had been crowned there by Joan of Arc on 17 July 1429, and the arrangements for Henry VI's coronation in England were hurriedly advanced; he was crowned in London on 6 November 1429, and it was proclaimed that he would go forthwith to France to be crowned in Reims; he eventually left on 23 April 1430 and was crowned, in Paris not Reims, on 16 December 1430. Lydgate wrote four poems associated with the London coronation: *A Prayer for King, Queen and People* (*MP*, I.212), asking God to preserve the "sixt Henry" (line 58), "hys moder Kateryne" (line 66) and the realm, and praying that God allow that Henry may "in short tyme" be crowned with two crowns, "First in this londe, and afterwarde in Fraunce" (line 81); a *Roundel for the Coronation of Henry VI* (*MP*, II.622); a *Ballade to King Henry VI upon his Coronation* (*MP*, II.624), said by Shirley (MS. Ashmole 59) to have been "presented" by Lydgate to the king on the day of his coronation; and the

29

verses on *The Soteltes at the Coronation Banquet of Henry VI* (*MP*, II.623), in which Lydgate explains how the banquet decoration reinforces the theme of the dual monarchy, under the dual aegis of St. Louis and St. Edward, St. Denys and St. George.[69]

It is hard to believe that Lydgate was not present on some or all of these occasions. Everything, it is true, could have been communicated to those who commissioned it without Lydgate being personally present, and the only external "evidence" of Lydgate's presence is that provided by Shirley for the *Ballade*. It is also very difficult to find comparable instances of a monk apparently in attendance upon the king or the royal household, or in any way "seconded" to the royal service. Ranulph Higden, monk of Chester and author of the *Polychronicon*, was summoned to court in 1352, to bring with him all his chronicles and to speak and take advice with the King's Council; John Kyngton, a monk of Christ Church, Canterbury, was brought to court in 1414 to explain the details of the previous king's truces with Prussia (he had been previously a clerk in that king's service); the author of the *Versus rhythmici de Henrico Quinto*, possibly a monk of Westminster, and the author of the *Liber metricus de Henrico Quinto*, Thomas Elmham, a monk of St. Augustine's, Canterbury, both seem to have had some personal acquaintance with Henry V, but there is no evidence of any attachment to his household.[70] What we must acknowledge is that Lydgate's career as a monk-poet-propagandist was altogether exceptional; it was so exceptional that it may have included journeyings and periods of residence in or about the royal household such as appear to be quite unprecedented.

With this period of intense activity for and around the royal court, and perhaps specifically with 14 February 1429, we may associate *A Valentine to her that excelleth all* (*MP*, I.304), in which Lydgate declares the Blessed Virgin Mary to be his Valentine's day choice for every year and commends Henry VI and his mother Katherine to the Virgin's care (line 136). One might also allow some credence to Shirley's statement that the poem *That now is Hay some-tyme was Grase* (*MP*, II.809) was made by Lydgate "at the commaundement of the Quene Kateryn as in here sportes she wallkyd by the medowes that were late mowen in the monthe of Iulij" (BL MS. Additional 29729). It is a nice thought (though the queen's "sportes" would not have been much enlivened by the three stanzas in which Lydgate reminds ladies that their beauty is doomed to decay, lines 41-64), but it could have occurred spontaneously to Shirley: the specificity has an air of authenticity, but it could have been invented to give just that air.

Mention should be made at this point too of the undated love-poems, so that they do not become irrevocably associated by default with Lydgate's early career (see note 9 above). It is likely that such poems were written during this period of comparatively close contact with the court, though Shirley's rubrics are as optimistically uninformative as they customarily are when he has no information: "une soynge moult plesaunt fait a la request dun amoreux par Lidegate le Moyngne de Bury," he says, concerning *The Temple of Glass* (in BL MS. Additional 16165), or "a balade whiche that Lydegate wrote at the request of a squyer that serued in loves court" (BL MS. Additional 29729), for *A Ballade of her that hath all the Virtues* (*MP*, II.379). Shirley finds considerable amusement in pretending to take Lydgate's comments *in alia persona* as if they really referred to the monk himself, writing for instance "Be stille daun Johan, suche is youre fortune" beside a poem (line 66) lamenting the disdain of the poet's mistress, *The Servant of Cupyde Forsaken* (*MP*, II.427) in BL MS. Additional 16165.

The London mummings of this period (1427-29) also encourage one to place here certain "London" poems. *Bycorne and Chychevache* (*MP*, II.433) is called by Shirley "the deuise of a peynted or desteyned clothe for an halle a parlour or a chaumbre deuysed by Iohan Lidegate at the request of a werthy citeseyn of London" (MS. Trinity R.3.20). *The Legend of St. George* (*MP*, I.145) was similarly "the devyse of a steyned halle" made by Lydgate for the Armourers of London and their feast of St. George. It was probably at this time too that he wrote *A Procession of Corpus Christi* (*MP*, I.35), "an ordenaunce of a precessyoun of the feste of corpus cristi made in london by daun John Lydegate" (MS. Trinity R.3.20). Whether Shirley has earned enough credibility to be believed when he says that *Gaude Virgo Mater Christi* (*MP*, I.288) was made by Lydgate "by night as he lay in his bedde at London" (MS. Trinity R.3.20), it is hard to say. Certainly, Bury had a town house in London, Bevis Marks, or "Buries Markes," chiefly to accommodate the abbot and his entourage when he was attending parliament;[71] it may have provided Lydgate with a pied-à-terre in the city.

Lydgate was also active during this period in responding to commissions from aristocratic patrons. *The Legend of St. Margaret* (*MP*, I.173) was written for "my lady Marche" (69), who first commanded him to search out the life in French and Latin and "thereof make a compilacyoun" (line 74). Anne (d. 1432), daughter of Edmund, fifth earl of Stafford (died at Shrewsbury, 1403), married in 1415 Edmund Mortimer, fifth earl of March (1391-1425). One might assume that Lydgate's poem was written for Anne before she remarried in 1427,[72] but she would continue to bear the more distinguished title after her remarriage: this is how one might make sense of the rubric in Durham MS. Cosin V.ii.14 which dates the poem to 8 Henry VI (1429-30).[73] Possibly linked with the commissioning of *St. Margaret* may be the *Invocation to Seynte Anne* (*MP*, I.130), which was written, Shirley tells us, "at the commaundemente of my Ladie Anne Countasse of Stafford" (MS. Ashmole 59). Anne (1379-1438) was the countess of March's mother.

One is tempted to see other links between Lydgate's commissions, for instance between Warwick's commissioning of *The Title and Pedigree* in 1426 and the poem on *The Fifteen Joys of Our Lady* (*MP*, I.260), said in a rubric in MS. Trinity R.3.21 copied by Stow to have been translated by Lydgate "at thinstance of the worshipfull Pryncesse Isabelle nowe Countasse of Warr [Warwick] lady Despenser." Isabel was the heiress in her own right of her father, Thomas, Lord le Despenser, earl of Gloucester (d. 1400), and the widow of Richard Beauchamp, earl of Worcester, slain at Meaux in 1422; she married Richard Beauchamp, earl of Warwick (d. 1439), before 1425. Stow's "nowe"—unless he put it in himself to give his rubric the impression of authentic contemporaneity —suggests a recent event, and a very appropriate date of 1425-26. The link with Warwick and 1426 is more tenuous in the case of *Guy of Warwick* (*MP*, II.516), written, says Shirley, "at the requeste of Margarite Countas of Shrowesbury Ladye Talbot fournyual and Lisle of the lyf of that moste worthy knyght Guy of Warwike, of whos bloode shee is lyneally descendid" (BL MS. Harley 7333). Margaret was the daughter of Richard Beauchamp, earl of Warwick, by his first wife Elizabeth (d. 1422), daughter of Thomas, lord Berkeley. Margaret married John, lord Talbot (d. 1453), in 1433; he became earl of Shrewsbury in 1442. Robinson (1899) argues that the commission must have been made after she became countess of Shrewsbury, but of course the rubric is later than the commission and would dignify her by whatever titles she subsequently came into. It is odd that there is no mention of her father, customarily regarded as the paragon of chivalry, in the poem.

Return to Bury, 1433-41

By 1430 Lydgate had given up the priorate at Hatfield, though he continued to reside there. Things were quiet while the king was in France (if Lydgate had been with him, we should be sure to have heard of it in poetic celebrations of the coronation in Paris), but not long after May 1431 Lydgate began, at the request of Humphrey, duke of Gloucester (see Prologue 428-34), his immense translation of *The Fall of Princes*, based on Laurent de Premierfait's version of Boccaccio's *De Casibus virorum illustrium*. Lydgate alludes in the Prologue (372-78) to Gloucester's lieutenancy in England during the absence of the king in France (April 1430 to February 1432) and also to his part in suppressing the Lollard risings of the spring of 1431 (Prologue 400-413).[74]

These were the years when Gloucester was at the height of his power and influence, and the commission to Lydgate was designed to advance the duke's reputation as a European patron of letters and as the English representative of the new Italian humanist learning. His plans came unstuck, partly because of Lydgate's inert response to the materials, and one suspects that Gloucester gradually lost interest.[75] The Prologue to Book III tells how weary and desperate Lydgate was at his slow progress, but how his lord revived him with his largesse (III.74). This presumably refers to an act of isolated munificence prompted by Lydgate's own *Letter to Gloucester* (*MP*, II.665), a separate poem written "ad Ducem Glowcestrie in tempore Translacionis libri Bochasij pro oportunitate pecunie" (BL MS. Additional 34360).[76] In this witty poem, Lydgate complains that he could find no apothecary to offer any tonic for his sickly purse, "Dragge nor dya was noon in Bury toun" (line 12).[77] Not to put too much stress on a passing reference, this does suggest that he was now back in Bury: one of the reasons he returned there was perhaps the need for security now that Gloucester's support had turned out to be so erratic. It is quite possible that the *Letter* was written to put pressure on Gloucester when he came to Bury during the royal visit of 1433-34.

By Book III, 3837-71, in his discussion of how poets have in the past had the support of great lords but not, it seems, now, Lydgate is again begging the "welle of fredom" to relieve his poverty and distress.[78] In the Prologue to Book VIII he complains about how worn-out and old he is, "Mor than thre score yeeris" (VIII.191). This would be around 1436, when he was about sixty-five. By the end of Book IX he is "ronne ferre in age" (IX.3313) and has been sustained in his weary task only by hope of his lord's generosity. He probably finished the poem around 1438.

But before this great labour was even well under way, Lydgate had been briefly recalled once more to the public service. Henry VI returned to London on 21 February 1432, having been almost two years away in France, and the civic authorities put on an elaborate allegorical tableau to welcome him and to proclaim the virtues of the city. The Lord Mayor, John Welles, wanted the event commemorated in verse and incorporated in the chronicles of the city, and he commissioned Lydgate to write up *King Henry VI's Triumphal Entry into London* (*MP*, II.630). Lydgate addresses the "noble Meir" at the end of the poem. It has been suggested that Lydgate had a part in the organisation of the proceedings, in collaboration with the main organiser, John Carpenter, Town Clerk of London, but MacCracken makes it clear that Lydgate for the most part merely versified the vivid and detailed description of the event given in an informal Latin letter from Carpenter to a brother-cleric, presumably Lydgate himself.[79] Lydgate offers some information that is not in Carpenter; gives an explanation of the allegorization of the Mayor's name in one of the displays, a detail that Carpenter (unaccountably) missed; and may possibly have been present.[80]

Lydgate was probably in Bury on a permanent basis by the time of the royal visit that was announced on 1 November 1433 and lasted from Christmas Eve 1433 to 23 April 1434, even though the *dimissio* to leave Hatfield and return to Bury was not recorded until 8 April 1434 (Appendix no. 12). The visit was a great event and an unusual (and expensive) honour for the abbey. The king took a full part in the life and services of the abbey, living in the prior's house for most of the time, with members of his household, and was admitted solemnly to the fraternity of the abbey, along with Warwick and Gloucester, before leaving. Abbot Curteys asked Lydgate, who was already of course well known to the young king, to provide an English version of the *vita* of St. Edmund to commemorate the visit, and the dedication copy of *The Lives of St. Edmund and St. Fremund* survives (BL MS. Harley 2278), a magnificent manuscript with 120 miniatures, probably made by a "school" of copyists and illuminators in or near Bury.[81] Lydgate tells us in the poem that he wrote at the request of abbot William (I.187), presumably for presentation to the king at some future date, since the visit is already over when Lydgate begins to write (I.186-92). The presentation picture in BL MS. Harley 2278 (f. 6) shows the presentation of the book to the king taking place in the abbey church, but the picture is not necessarily of a real past event, or of an event with a real book containing Lydgate's poem. The translation probably took him some time (he was still working on the *Fall*) and he speaks of his "speritis feeble and feynt with yeeris olde" at the beginning of Book III (III.80). He ends with a prayer to St. Edmund to pray for "thenheritour off Inglond and Ffraunce" (III.1457-1520) and a dedication to the king, beseeching him to accept the presentation of "this tretys" (III.1556-62). Later manuscripts contain additional miracles, probably written about 1444, and not by Lydgate.

The two poems beseeching the Virgin to turn away the plague, *Stella celi extirpavit* (*MP*, I.294, 295), may possibly be associated with 1434, which was a bad plague year. More precise is the occasion of two poems that allude to the unravelling of the Burgundian alliance in 1436. The peace conference at Arras called by Philip, duke of Burgundy, after the death of Bedford in 1435 ended with the duke's calling upon Henry VI to accept Normandy and renounce his claim to the French throne; the English walked out, and Philip went into alliance with Charles VII, forgiving him his part in his father's murder in 1419. Traditional hatreds were now given their head, and city mobs attacked Flemings in London. Duke Philip besieged Calais but, in an isolated triumph for English arms, was forced to retire. All these events are alluded to in *A Ballade in Despite of the Flemings* (*MP*, II.600), which rejoices scornfully in the duke's discomfiture at Calais; it was part of a propaganda campaign launched against the duke and his subjects by the English government and orchestrated by Gloucester, who evidently asked Lydgate to take time off from his labours on the *Fall* to help with the publicity.[82] There is further passing allusion to the events of 1436 in *The Debate of the Horse, Goose and Sheep* (*MP*, I.539), a poem in which each of the three animals argues its greater usefulness to man. The allusion comes when Horse, opposing Sheep's claim to be the emblem of peace, points out that the siege of Calais of 1436 was all due to wool, and the attempt of the proud duke of Burgundy to seize the Calais wool trade for Bruges and Ghent (lines 412-20).

Soon after completing the *Fall of Princes* in about 1438, Lydgate was called upon to exert himself once more on the fulfilment of a substantial commission. The final colophon to the copy of *St. Albon and St. Amphibalus* in BL MS. Lansdowne 99 says that the saints' lives were "translatid out of Frenssh and Latyn by Dan Iohn Lidgate at the request of Maistir Iohn Whethamsted Abbot of Saynt Albon the yeer of our Lord MCCCCXXXIX."[83] Lydgate describes the commission from Whethamstede in similar terms (I.883-903, also II.2077-87) and compliments the abbot on the appropriateness of his name to his reputation as a great gatherer of good things into encyclopaedias. The concluding prayer to St. Albon includes a plea that the saint should pray for Henry VI (III.1555-68); in the 1534 print of the poem made at St. Albans this was replaced by a prayer for Henry VIII, Anna (Anne Boleyn) and their daughter Elizabeth.[84] Payment to Lydgate of £3.6s.8d. for translating the poem is recorded in the Register of abbot Whethamstede (Appendix no. 13), while another St. Albans compilation refers to the sum of over £5 paid for the copying and illumination of the translation (Appendix no. 13a). Green (1980, p. 157) points out that the record of the payment to Lydgate is "the first English record of a specific payment for literary services." If there were any lingering doubt that it was quite customary for monks to receive payment as individuals (which of course

35

they were forbidden to do by their Rule), the authorisation of this payment by the abbot of one Benedictine house to a monk of another should suffice to remove it.

Another St. Albans link may have prompted the writing of *The Legend of St. Austin at Compton* (*MP*, I.193), a legend told as a warning to those who complain about paying tithes. The warning is associated with a prayer that holy church may be kept free of heresy, "Nor no darnel growe nor multeplye, / Nor no fals Cokkyl be medlyd with good corn" (lines 387-88). Opposition to tithes was often associated with Lollards, who are here referred to as "cockles" or tares amid the good corn, in a way that had become customary. Schirmer (1961, p. 160) suggests a date of around 1433 for the poem, but there may be a more specific occasion. About 1440 the St. Albans monk John Fornset, attending the Council of Basle, wrote a letter to abbot Curteys urging him to send a representative, since monastic exemptions were under constant attack from the bishops at the Council. They are working, he said, not only to do away with exemptions but to abolish the impropriations of tithes by monasteries.[85] The emergence of this issue as an immediate cause of concern may well have prompted Curteys to suggest that Lydgate write a poem on the subject.

In 1439, as he approached the age of seventy, Lydgate finally received the reward that he had long thought his due. In that year, on 22 April, letters patent record the grant to John Lydgate, monk of Bury, "for good service to the king's father and uncles now deceased, to Humphrey, duke of Gloucester, and to the king, of ten marks a year out of the ancient and petty customs, the subsidies on wool, hides and wool-fells and tunnage and poundage in the port of Ipswich" (Appendix no. 14). We know of no service to the king's uncles that Lydgate performed other than that to Gloucester, though his work for Warwick on *The Title and Pedigree* in 1426 was equally a service to the king's uncle, the duke of Bedford, Warwick's superior; records of other commissions may have been lost. But the phrasing of the grant may be the product of a bureaucratic desire for all-purpose inclusiveness, and be designed to make sure that any person in the royal administration, past or present, that Lydgate felt he had a claim on for services rendered would by this act be discharged of obligation. The exchequer authorised in 1440 the payment of the appropriate portion of the grant for the part-year to Easter 1440 from the Ipswich customs (Appendix no. 15).

Almost immediately, on 7 May 1440, the responsibility for the payment of the annuity was transferred by letters patent from the Ipswich customs to "the blanch farm and the fee, commonly called 'Waytefee,' in the counties of Norfolk and Suffolk" (Appendix nos. 16, 17).[86] This was a routine transfer of financial responsibility from one government revenue department to another. A few days later, on 10 May 1440, the abbot of Bury was ordered to pay to Lydgate the biannual instalments due on his annuity from the "Waytefee" of Norfolk and Suffolk (Appendix no. 18). It is not clear whether this was a way of transferring the immediate responsibility for the payment of the annuity from the crown to the abbey, or whether it was designed to overcome the reluctance of the abbot, to whom all incoming moneys would be formally assigned, to pay over such a large sum of money to one of his monks. Either way, there was a definite hitch in the arrangements for the payment of the annuity, and on 14 November 1441 Lydgate himself addressed a petition in English to the king, informing him that the letters patent of 7 May 1440 were not working to his benefit (i.e. he was not getting his money) and begging that new letters patent might be issued, authorising the payment of the annuity jointly to himself and to John Baret, esquire of Bury (Appendix no. 19). On 21 November 1441 the original letters patent were cancelled and new ones issued in favour of Lydgate and Baret (Appendix no. 20). On the same day orders were sent out to the sheriff of Norfolk and Suffolk (the two counties had the same sheriff) to pay to Lydgate and Baret for their lives and the life of the longer liver the sum of £7.13s.4d. a year from the farms and revenues of those counties (Appendix no. 21). On the same day retrospective authorisation went to the sheriff of Norfolk and Suffolk for the payment of the half-year from Easter to Michaelmas 1440 which had been held up by the problem with the letters patent (Appendix nos. 22, 23). Subsequent payments proceeded smoothly, and are recorded for the years ending at Michaelmas 1441, 1443, 1446, 1448 and 1449 (Appendix nos. 24-29).

The invalidity of the original letters patent I take to be attributable to the fact that they authorised payment to Lydgate personally. In the king's articles presented to the great chapter of the English Benedictines in 1421 there are strict injunctions recommended against the receipt of money-allowances by individual monks; they are to be received and administered by one monk, "unus fidelis dispensator commonachus."[87] This article was rejected by the chapter, on the grounds that such receipt of money, in certain well-defined cases, and with the permission of the abbot, was not against the Rule.[88] Accusations by visiting abbots or bishops that monks were receiving money payments were customarily answered with the defence that the money was in reality paid to the monastery as a whole.[89] Knowles makes it clear that in the fifteenth century more and more monks had administrative positions (perhaps as many as half the members of a large community) and more and more payments, in lieu of clothes, and for services, were paid to individual monks.[90] But this was a milder infraction, and in a somewhat different category from payments to individual monks from outside sources, and it is likely that in this particular case abbot Curteys stood firm and insisted that the annuity should be paid jointly to Lydgate and John Baret, the abbey treasurer, thereby giving the grant a cloak of respectability as well as ensuring that a portion of the proceeds was diverted from Lydgate to the more general good purposes of the abbey.

Baret (d. 1467) was a highly respected member of the Bury citizenry, who commissioned much work in local churches and left large quantities of property and possessions to relatives, servants and friends (the first bequests listed in his will are to the abbot, prior and several named monks of Bury).[91] As *camerarius* or *thesaurarius* to the abbey, he had many close contacts with the house and its abbot: he was on commission with the abbot on 26 March 1443, approved an expense sheet prepared by the abbot, received a grant to have a portable altar, and made arrangements in his will for the disposal of two silver collars of SS's, presumably given to him as a mark of honour after the visit of Henry VI in 1434.[92] Knowles points to the powerful lay element that was finding its way into the monastic economy and administration in the fifteenth century: houses retained important local landowners and businessmen in semi-honorary positions, as steward (*senescallus*), receiver (*receptor*) or professional auditor, thus helping to ensure their friendly support of the abbey's causes.[93] Baret was less a financial officer at Bury than a guarantor of financial probity, chosen from among the respectable and well-off laymen of the town, much like the lay treasurer who sits on the Council or Senate of a modern British university.

It may be that the immediacy of the response to Lydgate's request for new letters patent in 1441 was in some measure attributable to the duke of Suffolk, who, we are told, was the person who sponsored his petition (Appendix no. 19). The reference by Adam Moleyns to the part played by Suffolk does not look like a merely formal indication of his presence. William de la Pole, earl and later duke (1446) of Suffolk (1396-1450), had been growing in power during the 1430s and was now entering upon the period of his greatest influence, quite eclipsing Gloucester. He may have known Lydgate for some time, as we have seen, and both he and his wife Alice, daughter of Thomas Chaucer, were members of the fraternity of the abbey at Bury: Lydgate wrote *The Virtues of the Mass* (*MP*,

I.87) "ad rogatum domine Countesse de Suthefolchia" (Oxford, St. John's College MS. 56) at some point after their marriage in 1430. There is also a poem called "A Reproof to Lydgate" which has been plausibly ascribed to Suffolk on the basis of its association with other poems presumed to be by Suffolk in Bodleian Library MS. Fairfax 16.[94] It is a playful and witty rebuke to Lydgate for speaking ill of women and saying that love is but dotage, and it has a condescending air appropriate to a lord. It seems to refer to *The Fall of Princes* and may date from about 1440. It is entirely likely that Lydgate appealed to Suffolk in 1441 for help with his petition to the king.

Last days, 1441-49

Lydgate was now very old, and the few poems that can be ascribed to the 1440s are those in which the protestations of old age and feebleness of wit are more than usually appropriate. *The Testament of Dan John Lydgate,* which has already been spoken of for its description of the poet's youth, is most probably to be dated to this period, as is the *De Profundis* (*MP,* I.77), an explanation of the biblical canticle which he was charged to write "in myn oold dayes / By William Curteys" (lines 163-64) so that the text might be hung on the wall of the abbey church (line 168). It is an unusual way for Lydgate to refer to his abbot. *An Exposition of the Pater Noster* (*MP,* I.60) also exploits the topos of old age, as does *A Prayer in Old Age* (*MP,* I.20). Apart from these, and two poems mistakenly attributed to the poet,[95] there remains only *The Secrees of Old Philisoffres*, the work with which Lydgate was apparently engaged when he died. At the opening of the poem, a translation of a version of the *Secreta Secretorum*, a book of the governance of princes, he prays God to protect the king and make him prosperous, and begs the king to excuse his rude style in this compilation, which he has taken in hand "ffor tacomplysshe your co-maundement" (line 28). The lack of specificity suggests that Lydgate was simply translating the prologue to the work that he found in his sources.[96] At line 1491 of the translation, which reads, "Deth al consum-yth, which may nat be denyed," the rubricator adds, "here deyed this translator and nobil poete: and the yonge folowere gan his prologe on this wyse." Lydgate's part of the translation is so fragmentary and amorphous that the continuator could easily have rearranged the stanzas to produce these neatly appropriate *obiter dicta.*

The "yonge folowere" who took on the completion of the work was Benedict Burgh (*c.* 1413-1483), who seems to have made Lydgate's acquaintance during the late 1440s. He was vicar of Maldon, in Essex, when he was presented to the rectorship of Sandon in 1440 (vacant by 1444) and became rector of Hedingham Sibele, a Bourgchier living, in 1450, going on from there to a prosperous career in the church.[97] He was tutor to the Bourgchier family, and a devoted follower of Lydgate.[98] *A Letter to Lydgate*, a fulsome tribute to the poet, was evidently written before Burgh met him and in the hope of an introduction—"Now god, my maister, preserve yow longe on lyue / that yet I may be yowr prentice or I dye" (lines 36-37).[99] The poem is dated 11 December, with no reference to the year, and was "written at thabbey of bylegh chebri place" (line 43), that is, at Beeleigh abbey, near Maldon. Burgh evidently thought Lydgate was on his last legs; Hammond's assumption (1927, p. 188) that the *Letter*, since it refers to Maldon, must have been written before 1440, when Burgh acquired the rectorship of Sandon, is not needed; Burgh would not necessarily have given up the one when appointed to the other. Stow has a characteristically hopeful note to the *Letter*, informing us that it was written by "Master Burgh in the prays of Iohn Lidgate . . . booth dwelyng at wyndsor" (BL MS. Additional 29729). This looks like guesswork, based on the presumed reference to the king and the known involvement of both poets in the work. It is not known who commissioned Burgh to complete the work after Lydgate's death, if indeed it did not occur to him spontaneously to do so; it may conceivably have been the king, or possibly Lord Bourgchier.[100]

The last recorded authorisation for payment of Lydgate's annuity was for the year ending Michaelmas (29 September) 1449 (Appendix no. 29). In his poem of *Amoryus and Cleopes*, the poet John Metham, whose patron was Sir Miles Stapleton, sometime sheriff of Norfolk and Suffolk, speaks of "Ion Lydgate, sumtyme monke off Byry" (line 2192), and later, referring to Chaucer as well as Lydgate, says, "But nowe thei bothe be pasyd" (line 2198).[101] This suggests that Lydgate joined Chaucer only recently. Metham tells us that his poem was written in 27 Henry VI (lines 2175-76), that is, strictly speaking, 1 September 1448 to 31 August 1449, though he is probably using the regnal year to refer to the calendar year 1449. It is reasonably certain that Lydgate died in the last quarter of that year.[102]

Lydgate was no doubt buried at Bury, perhaps in the monks' cemetery, perhaps, because of his eminence, within the abbey church. Various epitaphs are associated with his tomb, probably none of them genuine. Bale's *Index*, compiled 1548-52, records information concerning nineteen poems by Lydgate deriving "Ex collectis Nicolai Brigam," and at the end of the list has an "Epitaphium Lydgate":

> Mortuus seclo, superis superstes,
> Hic iacet Lydgate, tumulatus vrna:
> Qui fuit quondam celebris Britanne
> Fama poesis.[103]

Brigham most probably composed these lines for the occasion, as he later composed a very similar epitaph for Chaucer when he had him reburied in Westminster Abbey in 1556,[104] and passed them with his other information to Bale. It is inconceivable that such an epitaph would have been composed in provincial England in the mid-fifteenth century or that it would have appeared on a monastic gravestone. A translation of this epitaph is quoted by Edward King in 1776:

> Dead to the world, yet living in the sky,
> Intombed in this urn doth Lydgate lie:
> In former times fam'd for his poetry
> All over England.[105]

King also quotes yet another Latin epitaph, supposedly the original inscription on Lydgate's tomb, citing Weever and Willis as his source:[106]

> Lidgate Cristolicon, Edmundum, Maro Britanus,
>   Boccasiousque viros psallit; et hic cinis est
> Haec tria praecipua opera fecit:—vij libros de
> Christo; librum de vita Sancti Edmundi; et
> Boccasium de viris illustribus; cum multis aliis.

Of the three references to poems, it will be seen, one mistakes the *Life of Our Lady* for a life of Christ. The epitaphs are the product, it would seem, of an impulse to manufacture funerary inscriptions for famous long-dead writers.

More material evidence is provided in the account given by King in 1776 of some digging among the ruins of the abbey at Bury which uncovered among other things a fragment "of a coarse, soft stone; and very probably a part of the tomb of the famous Poet Lidgate, or Lydgate, whose name is very legible on it."[107] King points out that the fragmentary inscription, in which the word "lidgate" is certainly very clear (but nearly everything else illegible), corresponds with neither the Latin nor the English given by Weever, and suspects that these epitaphs may not be genuinely old. King was an antiquarian notorious in his day for testiness and occasional unreliability (the account of his life in *DNB* is distinctly hostile), but there is no reason to doubt the authenticity of the find. There is no trace of the tombstone now at Bury.

No mention has been made in this account of Lydgate's life of large numbers of his shorter poems, since there are no means of dating them or relating them to the known events of his life. Lydgate tells us that he wrote *The Legend of Seynt Gile* (*MP*, I.161) because he was brought "a lytell bylle / Of greet devossioun by a cryature" (lines 27-28), who asked him to translate the life of St. Giles out of the Latin. When this happened, or who the "cryature" was, is not known. *The Epistle to Sibille* (*MP*, I.14), addressed by Lydgate to "my ladye which cleped is Cybille" (line 135), is plausibly associated by MacCracken with Lady Sibille Boys of Holm Hale, and he proposes the same lady ("or some other Suffolk dame") as the recipient of *The Treatise for Laundresses* (*MP*, II.723).[108] Lady Sibille was perhaps the model of a worthy matron running her estates and living a life of duty, but since she was widowed in 1421 and lived till 1456, the speculation is not of much help to the biographer. *The Dietary* (*MP*, II.703), Lydgate's most popular work, to judge by the number of surviving copies, cannot be dated or placed at any point in his career. Some dates are worse than no date at all: Thomas Wright calls *The Cok hath Lowe Shoone* (*MP*, II.813) "On the Truce of 1444" on the basis of some supposed allusions to the "covert fraude" that may be concealed in a "fals pees" (line 33). But "pees" here does not mean a political peace-treaty, and the allusion, though accepted by the modern historian of Henry VI's reign, is an illusion.[109]

NOTES

Full references for the works cited here and in the Appendix are found in the Bibliography, under Modern Editions and Secondary Sources.

[1] Schirmer 1961; Pearsall 1970; Ebin 1985.

[2] Parr 1952, pp. 253-58. Lydgate's astronomy is not as expert as Chaucer's, and Parr, in his datings of the poems, occasionally has to fudge the text in order to get the readings he needs. Lydgate also makes some elementary errors, as in bringing the sun into Aquarius in mid-December in *The Temple of Glass*, lines 4-7 (see note 9 below). But the date indicated in the elaborate *chronographia* of the *Thebes* Prologue is unambiguous.

[3] *Fall of Princes*, VIII.194-96; *Isopes Fabules* (*MP*, II.567), lines 31-32. See also *Fall of Princes*, IX.3431-35.

[4] The abbey held lands and jurisdiction in the village of Lydgate: see Dugdale, *Monasticon*, III.121, 165. For a history and description of the abbey, see further Arnold, *Memorials*; *VCH* (*S*), II.56-72; Schirmer 1961, pp. 8-23; Pearsall 1970, pp. 22-48. For accounts of Bury's exceptionally large library, see James 1895 and 1926.

[5] For discussion of the testamentary conventions employed in Lydgate's poem, see Boffey 1992, pp. 46-51.

[6] Knowles 1955, p. 231; see also pp. 231-33, 294-97.

[7] See Appendix, no. 2. Lydgate makes a point of calling attention to the abbey's franchise in his versification of the abbey charters, the *Cartae Versificatae*, in BL MS. Additional 14848, ff. 243-56 (printed in Arnold, *Memorials*, III.215-37), f. 250v.

[8] See BL MS. Cotton Tiberius B.ix, ff. 69v, 85v; Tuddenham was ordained priest by Braybrooke on 23 December 1396 (Guildhall Library MS. 9531/3). Knowles 1955, pp. 232-33, says that ordination to priest normally took place seven years after entry into the novitiate; this makes Lydgate's progress even more tardy.

[9] See Schick 1891, p. c (early date also for *Reason and Sensuality* and *The Temple of Glass*); Schirmer 1961, p. 31; Norton-Smith 1966, p. 161 (use of lover-persona argues for an early date). An early date has come to be assumed for *The Temple of Glass* (see e.g. Wilson 1975, p. 26; Davidoff 1983, p. 124) ever since the argument of MacCracken 1908 that it was made for the marriage of William Paston in 1420 was demolished by Moore 1912, pp. 193-94. Norton-Smith 1958 argues that the poem went through various stages of revision, but does not associate the process of revision with adaptation for any specific occasion. There is no way of dating the poem precisely: 1420-30 is most likely. The astronomy is impossible (Parr 1952, pp. 251-52).

[10] Appendix no. 8. The names are abbreviated because the document is a formulary and not a collection of "real" letters.

[11] See H. E. Salter, "Chancellors and Proctors of the University of Oxford," in Salter 1924, pp. 318-35 (332-33); also *BRUO*.

[12] For the fortunes of the Prince of Wales during this period, see McFarlane 1972, chapters 5 and 6, and McNiven 1987. On the career of Henry V more generally, see Harriss 1985, Allmand 1992.

[13] See R. B. Dobson, "The Religious Orders 1370-1540," in *HUO*, pp. 539-79 (546-48). Bury had five students there in 1441: see Pantin, *Chapters*, III.222.

[14] Dobson, "Religious Orders," p. 568.

[15] See Pearsall 1970, pp. 32-45.

[16] M. B. Parkes, "The Provision of Books," in *HUO*, pp. 407-83 (450).

[17] Emden, however (*BRUO*, p. 1185), does consider it a mark of ownership.

[18] For Gloucester College, see Galbraith 1924, Pantin, *Chapters*, and Knowles 1955, *passim*.

[19] See Pantin, *Chapters*, II.216 (visiting taverns), III.31-32 (holding suppers); see also Knowles 1955, p. 22. The freedom of monks to own property, including books, and the use of a private room, were privileges that Henry V specifically tried to curtail in his attempt to reform the order in 1421: see Pantin, *Chapters*, II.114, 120; Knowles 1955, pp. 184, 244.

[20] See T. A. R. Evans, "The Number, Origins and Careers of Scholars," in *HUO*, pp. 485-538 (508); Dobson, *HUO*, p. 566. In theory, according to the statutes of the provincial chapter of 1363, monks were "strictly forbidden to bring pressure to bear on their abbots, by means of letters from magnates, to have themselves sent to university and allowed to take degrees": see W. A. Pantin, "Gloucester College," *Oxoniensia* 11-12 (1946-47), 65-74 (69).

[21] Norton-Smith 1966, p. 195. Norton-Smith thinks that Lydgate may have been at Oxford as early as 1397. Green 1980, p. 88, considers briefly the "intriguing though perhaps remote possibility" that Lydgate may have been enrolled as a clerk of the Royal Chapel, that is, as a king's clerk. Though not completely without precedent (two monks appear as king's chaplains in 1313 and 1316, *CFR*, 1307-19, pp. 181, 306), it is indeed a remote possibility.

[22] For discussion of Shirley (c. 1376-1456) and his career, see Hammond 1907; Hammond 1927, pp. 191-97; Brusendorff 1925, pp. 207-36, 453-71; Doyle 1961; Pearsall 1970, pp. 73-75; Green 1980, pp. 131-33; Doyle 1983; Lerer 1993, pp. 117-46.

[23] See Lerer 1993, pp. 117-46.

[24] See Norton-Smith 1966, pp. 150-51; Pearsall 1992, pp. 18-19. For the history of the prince's relations with Lollardy, see McNiven 1987.

[25] See J. H. Fisher, "Chancery and the Emergence of Standard Written English in the Fifteenth Century," *Speculum* 52 (1977), 870-99; J. H. Fisher, "A Language Policy for Lancastrian England," *PMLA* 107 (1992), 1168-80; D. Pearsall, "Hoccleve's *Regement of Princes*: The Poetics of Royal Self-Representation," *Speculum* 69 (1994), 386-410.

[26] Schick 1891, p. cviii, says 1409-11; Parr 1971 says 1415-16; Lauritis 1961, p. 6, says 1421-22; while Norton-Smith 1966, p. 155, suggests after 1434.

[27] Lauritis 1961, p. 240.

[28] See Pearsall 1970, p. 286; Keiser 1991, p. 154.

[29] Lauritis 1961, p. 6.

[30] See Pearsall 1992, p. 20.

[31] Parr 1971. The internal references are I.2, II.1612, 1617-18, III.10, 1766-71, IV.1-11, VI.450-52.

[32] See Ruud 1926, pp. 12-13, 25-26, 87; Schirmer 1961, p. 234, adds, with no plausibility at all, Charles of Orleans.

[33] See Fisher, "A Language Policy" (cited in note 25 above); J. M. Bowers, "The House of Chaucer & Son: The Business of Lancastrian Canon-Formation," *Medieval Perspectives* (Proceedings of the Southeastern Medieval Association) 6 (1991), 135-43.

[34] See Pearsall 1970, p. 162; Green 1980, p. 220. Pycard was probably an official in the household of Edward, duke of York (d.1415): see Pearsall, "Hoccleve's *Regement of Princes*" (cited in note 25 above), n.29.

[35] See Ruud 1926, pp. 25-29; Hammond 1927, p. 79; Norton-Smith 1966, p. 119.

[36] See Knowles 1955, p. 274.

[37] See Knowles 1955, p. 184.

[38] See Pantin, *Chapters*, III.84-87.

[39] This is the person formerly referred to as "Boston of Bury": see R. H. Rouse, "Bostonus Buriensis and the Author of the *Catalogus Scriptorum Ecclesiae*," *Speculum* 41 (1966), 471-99. His inscription appears in the manuscript once in the possession of Lydgate (see Appendix no. 30).

[40] See *VCH* (*S*), II.71; Arnold, *Memorials*, III.259-60.

[41] See Rymer, *Foedera*, X.895-904 (item 24, p. 901); *Thebes*, ed. Erdmann and Ekwall, I.vii, II.8-9.

[42] Ayers 1958, p. 468 n.26, considers the tone of hopefulness conventional, but he takes insufficient account of the shattering impact of the news of Henry's death.

[43] The question of who took the initiative in these often delicate negotiations between poet and patron is examined in Blake 1985, especially (for Lydgate) pp. 283-87; see also Lerer 1993, p. 51.

[44] A poem sympathetic to Jacqueline written on this occasion, *A Complaint for my Lady of Gloucester* (*MP*, II.608), is ascribed to Lydgate by Shirley in MS. Trinity R.3.20, though MS. Ashmole 59, the other manuscript of the poem, also written by Shirley (after 1450), calls it "a pytous complaynt of a Chapellayne of my lordes of Gloucestre Humfrey." The metre and style are not Lydgate's, and it is inconceivable that he would say anything critical of Gloucester.

[45] See Rymer, *Foedera*, X.261.

[46] J. W. H. Atkins, in a review of MacCracken's edition of *The Serpent* in *MLR* 7 (1912), 253-54, argued for accepting it, but his arguments were decisively refuted by Mac-Cracken in *MLR* 8 (1913), 103-04.

[47] See *Newington Longeville Charters*, ed. H. E. Salter, Oxfordshire Record Society (Oxford 1921), pp. x, xliv.

[48] See Tanner 1748, p. 389. Tanner reports the election of William of Exeter as abbot in 1415 and the election of Lydgate as prior of Hatfield in 1423 as follows: "In monasterio vixit A. mccccxv, ubi electioni Gul. Excestr. adfuit. *Reg.* Gul. Excestr. f. 9. A.mccccxxiii mense Junio electus est prior de Hatfeld Brodhook. Ibid. f. 28." The first reference is accurate (see Appendix no. 9), but the second is incorrect. On the folio to which Tanner refers (now f. 201r, badly damaged, in MS. Cotton Tiberius B.ix), there appears a record concerning Thomas de Lidgate, monk of Bury, *celerarius*, and dated 1330 (twice); it is an older precedent, referring to the rights of Bury to the church at Mildenhall, gathered for record into the Register. For the priory at Hatfield Broad Oak, see *VCH* (*E*), II.207-10; Dugdale, *Monasticon*, IV.432-35.

[49] The record of the appointment of a new vicar at Hatfield Regis on 12 May 1423 mentions the subprior and convent of Hatfield Regis as if there were no prior: see the

Register of John Kempe, bishop of London 1422-25, in London, Guildhall Library MS. 9531/4, f. 208v.

[50] See *CPR* 7 Henry VI, m.22, in *Henry VI*, I.511. Lowndes (1884) refers to entries in the court rolls for the 1420s in which the prior is fined for a trespass by his cattle, for not repairing a fence, and not having a ditch secured (p. 147), but he makes it clear that Lydgate is not named. Lowndes gives no reference to his sources, except to say that they are deeds and charters, formerly at Barrington Hall, in his own possession, and allows some confusion to persist concerning the relationship of John Derham and John Denham: both names appear in the early records, but they are the same person. John Derham, rector of Canfield Parva, appears as the first witness in the charter of 1425 (Appendix no. 11).

[51] BL MS. Additional 5813, f. 145v. This MS was formerly Cole MS. xii: see the *Index to the Contents of the Cole MSS. in the British Museum* by G. J. Gray (Cambridge, 1912), and the handwritten description of Add. 5813 by Sir F. Madden in the Students' Room at the BL in the Catalogue of Additional MSS.

[52] For Canfield's election, see the Register of Robert FitzHugh, bishop of London 1431-36, in London, Guildhall Library MS. 9531/4, f. 269v.

[53] If this is a correct interpretation, then his situation was the opposite of that of Thomas Walsingham, the St. Albans historian, who had a brief period as prior of Wymondham (1394-97) but returned to St. Albans in order to continue his historical writing in the peace of the cloister (and with access to a good library): see V. H. Galbraith, "Thomas Walsingham and the Saint Albans Chronicle 1272-1422," *EHR* 47 (1932), 12-29 (25). Lydgate's kind of writing needed less in the way of a large library; one book at a time was enough for his purposes.

[54] See Mooney 1989, especially pp. 256-59. The "Later Redaction of the Same by Another Hand" (*MP*, II.717) has a much more complicated textual history than MacCracken indicates, and is not by Lydgate.

[55] See Rowe 1932; McKenna 1965, pp. 151-53; Griffiths 1981, pp. 217-19; Patterson 1993, pp. 89-93.

[56] *CPR, Henry VI*, p. 362; Griffiths 1981, p. 187.

[57] See Green 1980, p. 187; Patterson 1993, p. 89.

[58] If Shirley's information is correct, and not merely plausible fabrication, the request must have been communicated to Lydgate before Charles VI died.

[59] See the edition by Warren and White, pp. xxiv-xxv; also Seymour 1983.

[60] Stow, *Survey of London*, I.327; Hammond 1927, p. 125: *Danse*, ed. Warren and White, p. xxiii; Pearsall 1987.

[61] The inventory of Alice's effects on her death in 1466 includes a paper copy of "the pilgrymage translated by daune Iohn lydgate out of frensh" (Green 1978, p. 106), most likely a copy (though not a presentation copy) of the poem Lydgate wrote for her second husband.

[62] Salisbury's death, along with that of Henry V and the dukes of Clarence and Exeter, is made part of the topos of mutability in *A Thoroughfare of Woe* (*MP*, II.822), lines 104-27.

[63] See *Pilgrimage*, ed. Locock, Part 3, p. lxix*; Brusendorff 1925, pp. 469-71; Pearsall 1970, facing p. 166.

[64] For discussion, see Brusendorff 1925, pp. 468-71; Pearsall 1970, pp. 173-74; Walls 1977; Green 1978.

[65] The next London parliament opened on 22 September 1429, and a mumming on that occasion could hardly have failed to mention the forthcoming coronation of Henry VI on 6 November 1429. See also Withington 1918, I.106.

[66] John Brice was not in fact "Controller" (of the Royal Household) but the deputy controller, or *cofferarius regis*; he probably died at the siege of Louviers in 1431. See Green 1976.

[67] See Griffiths 1981, pp. 60-62. For Katherine's wealth and possessions, see the settlement made upon her on 9 December 1422 that is recorded in Rymer, *Foedera*, X.258.

[68] Rymer, *Foedera*, X.387.

[69] On these poems, see McKenna 1965, pp. 153-58.

[70] See J. Taylor, *The Universal Chronicle of Ranulph Higden* (Oxford 1966), p. 1; Devon 1837, p. 334, and Patent Roll, 29 July 1413 (*CPR, Henry V*, p. 107); *Memorials of Henry the Fifth, King of England*, ed. C. A. Cole, Rolls series 11 (London 1858).

[71] See Stow, *Survey of London*, I.146.

[72] John Holand, earl of Huntingdon, later duke of Exeter (1395-1447), was heavily fined by the crown on 6 March 1427 for having married the countess of March without a royal licence. See Nicolas, *Proceedings*, III.352-53; Griffiths 1981, p. 87.

[73] Shirley, in a "Table of Contents" copied by Stow in BL MS. Additional 29729, refers to the commissioning of the work by "my lady of huntyngeton" (line 49), now buried at St. Katherine's in London, that was "the contesse of the marche in hur tyme" (line 52). See Hammond 1927, pp. 196-97.

[74] See Hammond 1927, p. 443. Letters from the crown to the abbot and town of Bury speak of the dangers of Lollardy, the fears of a Lollard outbreak in Cambridgeshire, and the assiduity of Gloucester in putting down Lollards. The letter to abbot Curteys was probably written on 5 June 1431 and that to the town on 6 July 1431. See J. Gage, "Letters from King Henry VI to the Abbot of St. Edmundsbury and to the Alderman and Bailiffs of the Town, for the Suppression of the Lollards," *Archaeologia* 23 (1831), 340.

[75] Hammond 1927 ("Lydgate and Coluccio Salutati") gives an account of Gloucester's failure to interest Lydgate in a new work by the Italian humanist Coluccio Salutati. For further discussion of Gloucester as patron, see Pearsall 1970, pp. 223-54, and the references collected there.

[76] For this interpretation of the date and occasion of the *Letter*, see Hammond 1914; her view is better supported than that of Norton-Smith 1966, pp. 114-16, that the *Letter* was written after the completion of the *Fall*, an opinion he bases on verbal similarities between the *Letter* and the final envoy of the *Fall*.

[77] Whether because of this poem alone, or because of references in the Prologue to *Thebes* and elsewhere too, Lydgate was famously poor. Shirley makes reference frequently to his poverty: see Pearsall 1970, p. 229. The joke, of course, which Lydgate well understood, was that a monk was *supposed* to be poor. In fact, he was far from poor.

[78] It is actually quite daring, as Green 1980, p. 156, points out, for Lydgate to suggest that poets should be financially provided for like other professional men.

[79] MacCracken 1911, p. 100; see also Withington 1918, pp. 141-47; McKenna 1965, pp. 160-62; Kipling 1982, p. 25, n.13.

[80] MacCracken assumes that he was (1911, p. 96), and also that he may have been in the king's retinue returning from France (p. 99), which is highly unlikely.

[81] See Scott 1982; Doyle 1983, pp. 174-75.

[82] See Griffiths 1981, pp. 222-24, 444.

[83] The other four manuscripts have a variant version of this colophon after the final prayer to St. Albon (III.1499-1603), which does not appear in the Lansdowne MS. For John Whethamstede (d. 1465), abbot of St. Alban's 1420-40 and 1451-65, see Pearsall 1970, pp. 44-45, 283-84, and the references collected there.

[84] This polite little topical reference was unfortunate for the abbey, in the event; and unfortunate for Schirmer, who neglected to observe that Horstmann's text, which he was using, was based on the 1534 print, and proceeded to the fabrication of a supposed allusion by Lydgate to the marriage plans of Henry VI and Anna, daughter of the count of Armagnac. See the edition of *St. Albon* by Reinecke 1985, pp. 267-68; Schirmer 1961, p. 170.

[85] Arnold, *Memorials*, III.254-57.

[86] Steele, in the collection of Life-Records prefixed to his edition of the *Secrees*, refers to the new charge for the annuity as being upon "the proceeds of the farm of Waytefee" (p. xxv), which is misleading, if it suggests a place-name. "Waytefee," as the context indicates, is the English term for *alba firma* (*blanche ferme* in French and later in English, see *OED* s.v. blanch, a., sign. 3), meaning "quit-rent," rent paid by farmers in silver (hence "white") instead of services.

[87] Pantin, *Chapters*, II.113.

[88] Pantin, *Chapters*, II.118-19.

[89] Pantin, *Chapters*, III.288, 307.

[90] Knowles 1955, pp. 240-44.

[91] Baret's very long and detailed will, in English, is printed in full in *Wills and Inventories from the Registers of the Commissary of Bury St. Edmund's and the Archdeacon of Sudbury*, ed. S. Tymms, Camden Society 49 (1850), pp. 15-44. Amongst many other items, he left to his cousin John Cleye "my boke with the sege of Thebes in englysh" (p. 35). For Baret as the abbey treasurer, see pp. 233-38.

[92] See *CPR, Henry VI*, II.199; BL MS. Additional 7096 (Part 2 of the *Registrum Curteys*), ff. 182v, 130v; *Bury Wills*, p. 41.

[93] See Knowles 1955, pp. 284-85.

[94] See MacCracken 1911, "An English Friend"; also Hammond 1927, pp. 198-201 (Hammond is doubtful about the attribution to Suffolk).

[95] *The Verses for Queen Margaret's Entry into London* (1445) are not listed in MacCracken's account of the canon, and are conclusively rejected by Kipling 1982; the *Epitaphium Ducis Gloucestrie* (1447) is likewise to be dismissed (see MacCracken, *MP*, I.xl). For discussion of the canon of Lydgate's works, see MacCracken, *MP*, I.v-lviii; Hammond 1927, pp. 78-79, 99-101; Schirmer 1961, pp. 264-86; Pearsall 1970, pp. 77-79. For an addition to the canon of a poem rejected by MacCracken, see Edwards and Jenkins 1973.

[96] When Shirley made his prose translation (unfinished) of the *Secreta Secretorum* (BL MS. Additional 5467), he took the opportunity of these same lines to insert a dedication to Henry VI: see *Secrees*, ed. Steele, pp. xiii, 87.

[97] See Emden, *BRUO*, I.309; *Secrees*, ed. Steele, pp. xvii-xviii.

[98] Henry de Bourgchier, count of Ewe, and his son John were admitted to the fraternity of the abbey of Bury in 1440: see C. Ord, "Account of the Entertainment of King Henry the Sixth at the Abbey of Bury St. Edmund's," *Archaeologia* 15 (1806), 65-71.

[99] The poem is edited by Hammond 1927, pp. 188-90.

[100] See *Secrees*, ed. Steele, p. xvii.

[101] The poem is edited in *The Works of John Metham*, ed. Hardin Craig, EETS o.s. 132 (1916).

[102] Attempts to date his death later are mentioned in the article on Lydgate in *DNB*, which here as elsewhere is an Augean stable of misinformation, and are dismissed by MacCracken in his account of the canon in *MP*, I.xxxiii.

[103] See John Bale, *Index Britanniae Scriptorum*, ed. R. L. Poole and M. Bateson (1902), with a new introduction by C. Brett and J. P. Carley (Cambridge 1990), p. 231. The epitaph appears also in John Weever, *Ancient Funerall Monuments* (London 1631), p. 730.

[104] See D. Pearsall, "Chaucer's Tomb: The Politics of Reburial," *Medium Aevum* 64 (1995), 51-73 (esp. 59-63).

[105] Edward King, "An Account of the Great Seal of Ranulph Earl of Chester; and of Two Ancient Inscriptions found in the Ruins of St. Edmund Bury Abbey," *Archaeologia* 4 (1776), 119-31 (p. 131). This volume is incorrectly dated 1786 on the title-page.

[106] The epitaph is not to be found in Weever's *Ancient Funerall Monuments*, nor in any volume of Willis known to me.

[107] Edward King, *op. cit.*, pp. 129-30. A drawing of the inscription is included between pp. 130-31. In an earlier communication, "Remarks on the Abbey Church of Bury St. Edmund's in Suffolk," *Archaeologia* 3 (1775), 311-14, King described "a careful inspection of the foundations of the Ruins" that he had made in the summer of 1772. The discovery of the Lydgate tombstone was the result of subsequent searching by a Mr. Godbold in the grounds of his house, adjacent to the surviving ruins (see *Archaeologia* 4, pp. 119, 129).

[108] See MacCracken, *MP*, I.xix-xx.

[109] See Griffiths 1981, p. 490.

TABLE OF DATES*

c. 1371	Born at Lydgate, in Suffolk.
c. 1386	Enters novitiate at Bury St. Edmunds.
c. 1387	Makes profession of obedience.
1389 13 March	Ordained acolyte.
1389 18 Dec.	Ordained subdeacon.
1393 31 May	Ordained deacon.
1397 7 April	Ordained priest.
1406 × 1408	Studying at Oxford.
1412-20	*Troy Book* (begun 31 October 1412).
1413 20 March	Accession of Henry V.
1413	*A Defence of Holy Church* (after 20 March).
1414 × 1417	*Benedic anima meo* written at Windsor.
1414 or 1417	*Balade at the Departing of Thomas Chaucer.*
1415	At Bury for election of new abbot.
1415 × 1422	*The Life of Our Lady.*
1421-22	*The Siege of Thebes* (finished by 31 August).
1422	*On Gloucester's Approaching Marriage.*
1422 31 Aug.	Accession of Henry VI.
1422 (late)	*A Praise of Peace.*
1422 December	*The Serpent of Division.*

* The designation "×" means "happened between these 'ates but did not necessarily last as long as the period covered by the dates."

1423 21 Feb.	Lease to Lydgate of quarter-share in rents of Newington Longeville.
1423 June	Appointed prior of Hatfield Broad Oak.
1425 × 1426	*The Fifteen Joys of Our Lady.*
1426 (June?)	*The Kings of England sithen William Conqueror.*
1426 28 July	Begins *The Title and Pedigree of Henry VI.*
1426	In Paris, translates *Danse Macabre.*
1426-28	*Pilgrimage of the Life of Man.*
1427 Oct-Nov.	*Mumming at London.*
1427 25 Dec.	*Mumming at Hertford.*
1428 1 Jan.	*Ballade on a New Year's Gift.*
1428 25 Dec.	*Mumming at Eltham.*
1429 6 Jan.	*Mumming for Mercers of London.*
1429 2 Feb.	*Mumming for the Goldsmiths of London.*
1429	*A Prayer for King, Queen and People* (before 6 November).
1429 6 Nov.	*Ballade at the Coronation of Henry VI.* *The Soteltes at the Coronation of Henry VI.*
1429 × 1430	*The Legend of St. Margaret.*
1429 × 1430	No longer prior at Hatfield, but still resident there.
1430	*Danse Macabre* redone for John Carpenter
1431-38	*The Fall of Princes.*
1434 8 April	Formally released from obedience at Hatfield in order to return to Bury.
1434-36	*St. Edmund and St. Fremund.*
1436	*Ballade in Despite of the Flemings.*
1436-37	*Debate of the Horse, Goose and Sheep.*
1439	*St. Albon and St. Amphibalus.*

51

1439 23 April	Granted annuity payable from customs at Ipswich.
1440	Easter Payment of grant authorised for half-year.
1440 7 May	Responsibility for payment of grant made over to sheriff of Norfolk and Suffolk.
1440 10 May	Abbot of Bury ordered to pay Lydgate his grant.
1441 14 Nov.	Petitions for new letters patent.
1441 21 Nov.	New letters patent granted; payment to be made jointly to Lydgate and John Baret.
1441 21 Nov.	Instructions issued for payment of new grant.
1441 21 Nov.	Back-payment authorised for Easter-Michaelmas 1440.
1441	Record of payment of grant for year to Michaelmas.
1443	Record of payment of grant for year to Michaelmas.
1446 2 Oct.	Receipt of Baret for half-year's payment.
1448	Record of payment of grant for year to Michaelmas.
1449	Record of payment of grant for year to Michaelmas.
1440 × 1449	*De Profundis; The Testament of Dan John Lydgate.*
1449	*The Secrees of Old Philisoffres.*
1449	Dies, after 29 September and before the new year.

Documents Relating to Lydgate

There are brief references to a few of the following records in Tanner 1748, pp. 489-93; *DNB*; Schick 1891, pp. lxxxv-cxiii; *BRUO*; Schirmer 1961, p. 21 (Schirmer quotes here from a note in Hortis 1879, p. 641, n. 2, deriving from a manuscript note in Tyrwhitt's copy of Wayland's print of *The Fall of Princes*, now BL 838 m. 17), pp. 246-47; Norton-Smith 1966, pp. xiii-xv. Steele 1894, Appendix I, pp. xxiii-xxx, prints twelve of the records in full, and two others have been printed elsewhere, as indicated in the headnotes to these items. All (except items 15 and 27, as explained in the headnotes to those two items) have been reexamined against the original sources. The remainder are newly transcribed from those and other original sources, and printed here for the first time. I am grateful to Professor David Smith, of the Borthwick Institute for Historical Research in the University of York, for his generous help with problems in the transcribing of the Latin.

NOTE: Square brackets are used for editorial insertions and editorial omissions (summarized in italics), and for lost or illegible letters (dots) and tentative supply of such letters (roman). Pointed brackets (<>) are used for conjectural supply of lost letters; round brackets are used for interlinear insertions. All abbreviations are expanded; punctuation, where supplied by previous editors, is modern, but capitalisation is original.

1. LYDGATE ADMITTED TO THE ORDER OF ACOLYTE IN HADHAM CHURCH, 13 MARCH 1388 (i.e. 1389). Register of Robert Braybrooke, bishop of London 1381-1404: Guildhall Library, London, MS. 9531/3, f. 19r2.

Ordines celebrati in ecclesia parochiali de Hadham / Londoniensis diocesis per Reuerendum in christo patrem et dominum / dominum Robertum dei gratia Londoniensis Episcopum die sabbati / quatuor temporum in prima ebdomada quadragesima / videlicet die xiijma mensis marcij Anno domini millesimo / cccmo Octuagesimo octauo Et consecrationis dicti Reuerendi patris anno octauo. / Accoliti quicumque / [*eight names*] / Iohannes Lidgate / Thomas Osberne / Henricus Methewold / [*on left*] fratres / [*on right*] monachi monasterii de Bury / ordinis sancti Benedicti Norwicensis diocesis per literas dimissorias ad omnes. [*Subdeacons, etc., follow on verso.*]

2. LETTERS DIMISSORY FOR LYDGATE'S ADMISSION TO THE ORDER OF SUB-DEACON, 17 [DECEMBER] 1389. Register of William de Cratfield, abbot of Bury 1390-1415: London, BL MS. Cotton Tiberius B.ix, f.35v. The MS was damaged in the Cotton fire, and the edges of this page are split and shrivelled badly; [December] being now illegible is from Tanner 1748, p. 489.

Reuerendis in christo patribus ac dominis dominis Wintoniensi Eliensi Londoniensi <episcopis prouincie An> / glie ac cuiuslibet eorum suffraganeis. Willelmus permissione diuina Abbas monasterii sancti Edmundi / de Bury ad Romanam ecclesiam nullo medio pertinentis reuerenciam tantis patribus debitur cum / honore. Cum nobis et monasterio nostro predicto a sede apostolica specialiter sit indultum quod cuicumque / Episcopo catholico execucionem sui officii optinenti commonachos nostros dicti monasterii ac sacerdotes / de Bury iurisdiccionis nostre exempte existentes per nos legitime dimissos ad omnes / ordines licen[..] ordinare vestris reuerendis paternitatibus fratres Willelmum Leyston Johannem Spal / dyng Johannem Melforth ad ordinem sacerdocij Thomam Osbern Henricum Medewold ad / ordinem diaconatus et Johannem Lydgate ad ordinem subdiaconatus commonachos et con / fratres nostros professos presentamus per presentes humiliter supplicantes quatinus eosdem confratres / nostros ad dictos ordines dignemini promouere. Quilibet que vestrum prefatis Willelmo Johanni / Johanni Thome Henrico Johanni ordines predictos conferendi eisque prefatos ordines a quibus / [....<ten>]ore presentium concedimus facultatem In cuius rei / [...<testimonium>..<D>]ata in monasterio nostro predicto xvij die [<Decembris>...] lxxxixno.

3. LYDGATE ORDAINED SUBDEACON BY JOHN FORDHAM, BISHOP OF ELY, 18 DECEMBER 1389. Register of John Fordham, bishop of Ely 1388-1425: Cambridge UL, EDR [Ely Diocesan Records] G/1/3, f. 231r1.

Ordines celebrati per Reuerendum supradictum patrem / in capella manerij sui de dounham die sabati quatuor / temporum proximum post festum sancte lucie virginis videlicet / xviij die mensis decembri anno domini supradicto / [*admissions Ad primam tonsuram* / *Accoliti*] *subdiaconi* / Thomas lydegate monachus de Bury / Thomas Wyot de Burwell [*etc.*].

4. LETTERS DIMISSORY FOR LYDGATE'S ADMISSION TO THE ORDER OF DEACON, 28 MAY 1393. London, BL MS. Cotton Tiberius B.ix, f. 69v.

Memorandum quod dominus Abbas contulit literas dimissorias dompnis Roberto Pynchebek ad ordinem / sacerdocij Johanni Lydgate Johanni Wedyrden Johanni Corton ad ordinem diaconatus / Willelmo Lyndon ad ordinem subdiaconatus Ricardo Hopton Ricardo Ormysby et Johanni / Tudenham ad ordinem accolitatus sub dato xxviijo die Mensis Maii Anno domini Millesimo ccc Nonogesimo tercio.

5. LYDGATE ORDAINED DEACON IN THE CHAPEL OF THE MANOR AT DOWNHAM BY THE BISHOP OF ELY, 31 MAY 1393. Register of John Fordham, bishop of Ely: Cambridge UL, EDR [Ely Diocesan Records] G/1/3, f. 234r1.

Ordines celebrati per Reuerendum in christo patrem dominum Johannem / dei gratia Episcopum Eliensis in capella maiori manerij / sui de dounham die sabati in quatuor temporum in septima / nana [*sic*] pentecostis videlicet vltimo die mensis Maij / anno domini Millesimo cccmo nonagesimo tercio. / [*admissions Ad primam tonsuram, Accoliti, Subdiaconi follow*] / diaçoni / [*three monks from Ely*] / frater Iohannes Lidgate / frater Iohannes Wetherden / Iohannes Corton / [*on right*] monachi de Bury / [*etc.*].

6. LETTERS DIMISSORY FOR LYDGATE'S ADMISSION TO THE ORDER OF PRIEST, 4 APRIL 1397. London, BL MS. Cotton Tiberius B.ix, f. 85v.

Memorandum quod dominus Johannes Goseforth Prior contulit literas dimissorias dompnis Johanni Lydgat[.] / Willelmo Lyndon Ricardo Ormysby Johanni Gedeneye Johanni Charlys ad ordinem sacerdocii / Johanni Hornynggeshthe [*sic*] Henrico Herin Henrico Notyngham ad ordinem diaconatus / Johanni Burgh ad ordinem subdiaconatus Johanni Lynne et Johanni Heygham ad ordinem accolitatus sub dato iiijto die mensis Aprilis Anno domini Millesimo cccmo / Nonogesimo septimo.

7. LYDGATE ORDAINED PRIEST IN THE CHAPEL OF THE MANOR OF DOWNHAM BY THE BISHOP OF ELY, 7 APRIL 1397. Register of John Fordham, bishop of Ely: Cambridge UL, EDR G/1/3, ff. 237v2-38r1.

Ordines celebrati per Reuerendum in christo patrem dominum / Iohannem dei gratia Episcopum Eliensis in capella / maiori manerij sui de dounham die sabbati / qua cantatur officium sicientes videlicet vij die / mensis Aprilis anno domini Millesimo cccmo nonagesimo / septimo. / [admissions Ad primam tonsuram, Accoliti / f. 238r1 / Subdiaconi, diaconi] presbiteri / Rogerus Grey [etc.] / frater Iohannes Lydgate / frater Willelmus Lyndon / frater Ricardus Ormesby / frater Iohannes Gedeneye / frater Iohannes Charles / [on right] monachi de Bury / [etc.].

8. THE PRINCE OF WALES WRITES TO THE ABBOT AND CHAPTER OF BURY REQUESTING THAT DAN J. L. BE GIVEN LEAVE TO CONTINUE HIS STUDIES AT OXFORD, c. 1406-8. Oxford, All Souls' College, MS. 182. f. 345r3-4. Printed in M. Dominica Legge (ed.), Anglo-Norman Letters and Petitions from All Souls MS. 182, Anglo-Norman Text Society, No. 3 (Oxford, 1941), No. 347, pp. 411-12.

Reverent pere en Dieu, et noz treschiers en Dieu, Nous vous saluons tressovent. Et pour ce que nous sumes par nostre treschier Cousin et clerc, M[estre] R. C., Chanceller d'Oxenford, et diverses aultres noz treschiers serviteurs continuelment entour nous esteantz enformez si-bien de les scen, vertue et bonne conversacion de nostre treschier en dieu dan J. L., vostre commoigne, come del grand desir qu'il ad a continuer a les Escoles, et mesmes noz cousin et serviteurs nous ont suppliez de vous escrire et prier pour vostre comun assent ottroier que le dit J. pourra continuer a les Escoles susdites, Si vous prions entere-ment et de cuer que a le dit J. par vostre comun assent vuillez granter continuance as dites Escoles a tielle pension comme ses aultres con-freres y preignent illoeques pour leur sustenance, tanque il pourra resonablement venir a perfeccion de science, par ensi que mesme celui J. soit de bonne conversacion et diligent pour apprendre, luy donantz aussi congie et eleccion d'estudier en divinitee ou en loy canoun a son plesir, et ce le plus favorablement a cause de nous, si que il pourra sentir mesmes cestes noz prieres lui valoir devers vous. En laquelle chose faisantz nous vous fer / rez grand plesir par ont vous nous trouverez le plus enclinez de vous moustrer bon seignurie es choses que vous avarez affaire pardevers nous en temps a venir. Nostre seignur vous garde ou bon gouvernement de sa seint religion. Donne, etc., de par le prince a l'abbe et Covent de Bury.

9. LYDGATE AT BURY FOR THE ELECTION OF THE NEW ABBOT, 28 JUNE 1415. Register of William of Exeter: London, BL MS. Cotton Tiberius B.ix, f. 182r (f. 9 in the old numbering of this section of the Cratfield/Exeter Register). Much damaged by fire.

[*Gives recognition to those monks present, in the order of their date of profession, at the election of the new abbot upon the death of*] bone memorie fratris Willelmi Cratf[...] / vicesimo octauo die mensis Junii Anno domini infrascript[.] / [*etc. etc., namely*] Roberto Iklyngham Priore Waltero Norwiche Willelmo Notyngham / S[...]lo Bray Petro Houton Thoma Plumpton Willelmo Barwe Ricardo Harde[graue] / Willelmo Excetre Johanne Saxham Thoma Ikworthe Ricardo Wysbeche Nicholao / Tymworth Johanne Kenynghale Willelmo Wytlyseye Johanne Plumstede Willelmo Laystone / Johanne Somers[l?]yn Johanne Lydgate Johanne Spaldyng Henrico Methewold Roberto Pynche / bek Johanne Wederdene Johanne Corton Willelmo Lyndon Thoma Syluer Ricardo Hop / ton Johanne Todenham Johanne Gedney Johanne Hornyngsherth Henrico Herinne Johanne / Charles Johanne Heygham Henrico Notyngham Roberto de Wesenham Johanne Crane / wys Willelmo Sewale Johanne Bonefant Galfrido Gunthorp Thoma Boston / Andrea Aston Willelmo G[...]dener Willelmo Curteys Simone Pynchebek Thoma / Cambrigge Johanne Dag[...]worth Johanne Colchestre Thoma Geddyng Willelmo Tynworth / (f. 182v) [....]o Northampton Willelmo Aston [....] / [...iton?] Willelmo Fowleden monachis [*etc.*].

10. LEASE TO LYDGATE AND OTHERS OF THE LANDS AND RENTS OF THE ALIEN PRIORY OF LONGVILLE HELD BY SIR RALPH ROCHEFORT, 21 FEBRUARY 1423. London, BL MS. Cotton Cleopatra F. iv, f. 7. No. II in Steele, after Nicolas 1834, III.40.

xxjo die Februarij anno primo apud Westmonasterium, presentibus dominis Ducibus Gloucestrie et Exonie [*etc.*], concessum erat quod omnia terre et tenementa pertinencia prioratui Sancte Fidis de Longville (alienigene alias dicto prioratui de Longville Gifford, alias dicto prioratui de Newenton Longville) cum pertinenciis in regno Anglie una cum omnibus aliis maneriis, terris [*etc.*], et pensione de Spaldyng valoris xl.li. per annum Abbathie de Aungiers, dudum pertinentibus secundum formam et effectum literarum patencium dominorum Henrici quarti et

Henrici quinti Regum Anglie Radulpho Rocheford militi inde con-
cessarum et confirmatarum dimittantur, modo ad firmam Dompno
Johanni Lidgate et Johanni de Tofte monachis, Johanni Glaston et
Willelmo Malton capellanis ad nominacionem prefati Radulphi
Rocheford sine aliquo inde reddendo, quousque dicto Radulpho provi-
sum fuerit de recompensa conveniente ad terminum vite sue ad valorem
annuum terrarum et tenementorum predictorum, prout sibi promissum
fuit per dominum Regem defunctum patrem Regis nunc apud Dovorr'.

11. A GRANT BY JOHN CLERK AND OTHERS CONFIRMING A
PAYMENT TO JOHN LYDGATE, PRIOR OF HATFIELD REGIS, OF 4d.
ANNUAL RENT FOR A TENEMENT AT BUSH END, HATFIELD, 25
MARCH 1425. London, BL Charter Addit. 28613.

Sciant presentes et futuri quod Nos Johannes Clerk de Hatfeld Regis
Simon Doom Ricardus Gardener et Thomas Goos de eadem dedimus
concessimus et hac presenti Carta nostra confirmauimus Johanni Lydgate Priori de Hatfeld Regis et eiusdem loci conventui quattuor denarios annui redditus ad duos anni terminos videlicet ad Festa Pasche et
sancti Michaelis per equales porciones [*etc.*] In cuius rei testimonium
huic presenti carte nostre Sigilla nostra apposuimus. hijs testibus Johanne Derham Rectore de Canefeld parua Willelmo Tansfeld Barbour de
Hatfeld predicta. Johanne Baryngton Junior Ricardo Palmere Junior de
eadem. Roberto Lambard et alijs Data apud Hatfeld predicta in Festo
Annunciacionis Beate Marie Virginis Anno regni Regis Henrici sexti
post conquestum tercio.

12. LYDGATE RECEIVES PERMISSION FROM THE PRIOR OF HAT-
FIELD TO RETURN TO LIVE AT BURY, 8 APRIL 1434. Registrum
Curteys, Part 1: BL MS. Addit. 14848, f. 108v (old numbering f. 90v).

Dimissio Johannis Lydgate monachi
ab obedientia Prioris de Hatfeld.

Johannes Prior Prioratus de Hatfeld Brodoke ordinis nigrorum Mon-
achorum, Londoniensis diocesis, fratri Johanni Lydgate Commonacho
et Confratri nostro, salutem et sinceram in Domino caritatem; Licet in
Prioratu nostro predicto habitu regulari aliquandiu fueris conversatus,
tamen cum, vt asseris propter frugem melioris vite captandam, ex certis
causis veris et legitimis conscientiam tuam in hac parte mouentibus, ad
Monasterium de Bury sancti Edmundi, in quo dictum dudum ordinem
legitime et expresse fueras professus, regressum habere proponas; Nos
qui commissarum nobis animarum salutem feruenti desiderio perop-

tamus, vt ad dictum Monasterium vel alibi in loco eiusdem religionis congruo et honesto, sumptis pennis cum Maria contemplationis libere valeas conuolare licenciam in domino tibi concedimus specialem. In cuius rei testimonium presentibus sigillum nostrum commune apposuimus. Data apud Hatfeld predicta viiio die Mensis Aprilis, Anno domini Millesimo ccccmo. xxxiiijto.

13. THE ABBOT OF ST ALBANS PAYS A MONK OF BURY FOR WRITING *THE LIFE OF ST. ALBAN*. Extraordinary expenses incurred by abbot John Whethamstede during the period of his first abbacy 1420-40, in BL MS. Arundel 34 (Register of the Abbots John Whethamstede and Thomas Ramryge), f. 67r (f. 66r in the old numbering).

Item, cuidam monacho de Burgo Sancti Edmundi, propter translacionem vite sancti Albani in nostrum vulgare

iij.li.vi.s.viii.d.

13A. ANOTHER RECORD OF THE SAME. BL MS. Cotton Nero D.vii (an illustrated compilation of lists of names of kings and popes, and abbots, priors and monks of St. Albans, with the deeds of Abbot Whethamstede listed ff. 27-35), f. 32r.

Item idem Abbas suis in temporibus traduci siue transfer / ri fecit in vulgare nostrum vitam sancti Albani martiris. in / modoque transferendi posuit huiusmodi ordinem. quod pro / nunc nullicubi infra Regnum sit vita ea accepcior ad legen / dum. Et circa hanc translacionem. scripturam libri et ap / paratum; expendisse fertur ultra summam centum soli / dorum.

14. A GRANT FOR LIFE TO LYDGATE, FOR GOOD SERVICE TO THE KING'S FATHER AND UNCLES NOW DECEASED, TO HUMPHREY, DUKE OF GLOUCESTER, AND TO THE KING, OF 10 MARKS FROM THE CUSTOMS AT IPSWICH, 22 APRIL 1439. Patent Roll, 17 Henry VI, Part 1 (*CPR, Henry VI*, Vol. III, HMSO 1907, p. 256): London, PRO C. 66/443, m. 7. No. III in Steele.

Pro Johanne Lydgate Monacho [*in left margin*]

Rex Omnibus ad quos etc. salutem. Sciatis quod de gracia nostra speciali, ac pro bono et gratuito seruicio quod dilectus nobis Johannes Lydgate, Monachus Monasterij siue Abbathie de Bury Sancti Edmundi, tam Carissimo Domino et Patri nostro ac Auunculis nostris defunctis quam nobis et carissimo Auunculo nostro Humfrido Duci Gloucestrie adhuc superstiti ante hec tempora multipliciter impendit, concessimus eidem Johanni decem marcas percipiendas annuatim, pro termino vite sue, tam de antiqua et parua custumis nostris, quam de subsidio lanarum coriorum et pellium lanutarum, necnon de subsidio trium solidorum de dolio et duodecim denariorum de libra, in portu ville Gippeswici per manus Custumariorum siue Collectorum custumarum et subsidiorum predictorum in portu predicto pro tempore existencium, ad terminos Sancti Michaelis et Pasche, per equales porciones. In cuius etc. Teste Rege apud Castrum suum de Wyndesore, xxij die Aprilis.

per breue de priuato sigillo.

15. ALLOWANCE OF PAYMENT OF THE 1439 GRANT, 6*l.*4*s.*5¼*d.* BEING THE PROPORTION DUE TO EASTER 1440. Enrolled Accounts, Exchequer (Lord Treasurer's Remembrancer), Customs, No. 20. Account of Walter Green and Thomas West, Collectors of Customs and Subsidies in the Port of Ipswich, from Michaelmas, 18 Henry VI, to Michaelmas, 19 Henry VI. No. IV in Steele. Not located in the present search.

Et Johanni Lyddegate Monacho Monasterij siue Abbathie de Bury Sancti Edmundi, cui Rex xxijdo. die Aprilis, Anno decimo septimo, concessit decem marcas....[*as in Document 14*]... porciones, videlicet de huiusmodi .x. marcis per annum a predicto .xxmo ijdo. die Aprilis dicto Anno. xvijmo.—vsque festum Pasche proximo sequentem Anno .xviijuo. vi.li. iiij.s. v.d. quarta. per breue Regis irrotulatum in Memorandis de anno .xixno. Regis huius termino Sancti Hillarij. Rotulo .xmo. et literas patentes ipsius Johannis de recepcione.

16. PAYMENT OF THE 1439 GRANT TRANSFERRED FROM THE IPSWICH CUSTOMS TO THE BLANCH FARM AND FEE IN NORFOLK AND SUFFOLK AS FROM EASTER 1440, 7 MAY 1440. Patent Roll, 18 Henry VI, Part 2 (*CPR, Henry VI*, Vol. III, p. 402): London, PRO C.66/466, m. 5. No. V in Steele.

Pro Johanne Lydgate Monacho [*in left margin*]

Rex Omnibus ad quos etc. salutem. Sciatis quod cum Johannes Lydgate Monachus de Bury Sancti Edmundi habens ex concessione nostra decem marcas percipiendas annuatim durante vita sua de custumis de Ippeswych per manus Custumariorum ibidem pro tempore existencium prout in literis nostris patentibus inde confectis plenius apparet in voluntate existat easdem literas in Cancellariam nostram restituere cancellandas ad effectum quod nos eidem Johanni septem libras tresdecim solidos et quatuor denarios percipiendos annuatim pro termino vite sue de exitibus et proficuis de alba firma et feodo vulgariter nuncupato Waytefee, in Comitatibus Norffolcie et Suffolcie, concedere dignaremur. Nos, de gracia nostra speciali, ac pro eo quod idem Johannes dictas literas nostras in Cancellariam nostram restituit cancellandus, concessimus eidem Johanni dictos septem libras tresdecim solidos et quatuor denarios percipiendos annuatim, durante vita sua, a festo Pasche vltimo preterito, de exitibus et proficuis prouenientibus de alba firma et feodo vulgariter nuncupato Waytefee predicto, per manus Abbatis de Bury Sancti Edmundi pro tempore existentis, et sic deinceps ad terminos Sancti Michaelis et Pasche per equales porciones durante vita sua predicta. In cuius etc. Teste Rege, apud Westmonasterium vij die Maij.

per ipsum Regem.

17. A SUMMARY OF THE ABOVE GRANT SENT TO THE EXCHEQUER FOR RECORD, 7 MAY 1440. Originalia Rolls, 18 Henry VI: PRO (E.371) IND. 1.6950, piece 2v.

Rex vij. die maij concessit Johanni Lydgate Monacho de / Bury sancti Edmundi .vij.li xiijs. iiijd. percipiendos annuatim / durante vita sua a festo pasche vltimo preterito de exitibus / et proficuis de alba firma et feodo vulgariter nuncupato / Waytefe in Comitatibus Norffolcie et Suffolcie per manus Abbatis de Bury / etc. reuersione ad Regem spectante. rotulo xvjo.

18. THE ABBOT OF BURY ORDERED TO PAY LYDGATE HIS ANNUITY, 10 MAY 1440. Close Roll, 18 Henry VI (CCR, Henry VI, Vol. 3, 1435-41, HMSO 1937, p. 314): London, PRO C.54/290, m. 13.

Pro Johanne Lydgate monacho. [in left margin]

Rex dilecto sibi in christo Abbati de Bury sancti Edmundi qui nunc est vel qui pro tempore fuerit. salutem Cum septimo die Maij vltimo preterito de gracia nostra / speciali per literas nostras patentes concesserimus Johanni Lydgate monacho de Bury sancti Edmundi septem libras tresdecim solidos et quatuor denarios / percipiendos annuatim durante vita sua a festo Pasche vltimo preterito de exitibus et proficuis prouenientibus de Alba firma et feodo vulgariter nuncupato / Waytefee per manus predicti Abbatis pro tempore existentis et sic deinceps ad terminos sancti Michaelis et Pasche per equales porciones durante vita ipsius / Johannis prout in literis predictis plenius continetur Vos mandamus quod eidem Johanni dictos septem libras tresdecim solidos et quatuor denarios annuos exnunc singulis annis ad terminos predictos de exitibus et proficuis prouenientibus de Alba firma et feodo vulgariter nuncupato Waytefee predicta soluatis iuxta / tenorem literarum nostrarum predictarum Recipientes a prefato Johanne de tempore in tempus literas suas acquietancie que pro nobis sufficientes fuerint in hac / parte per quas et presens mandatum nostrum vobis inde in compoto vestro ad Scaccarium nostrum de tempore in tempus debitam allocacionem habere faciemus Teste Rege apud Westmonasterium x die Maij.

19. PETITION OF LYDGATE TOUCHING THE INVALIDITY OF LETTERS PATENT GRANTING HIM 7*l*.13*s*.4*d*. YEARLY, AND PRAYING NEW LETTERS PATENT TO HIM AND JOHN BARET. GRANTED, 14 NOVEMBER 1441. London, PRO SC.8/248, item 12382. No. VII in Steele, after Nicolas 1834, V.156, after BL Addit. 4609, f. 64r, art. 27 (an eighteenth-century transcript).

Vnto the king oure most gratious soveraign lord.

Besechith you mekely youre pouere and perpetuell oratour Johnn Lydgate monke of Bury seint Edmund. For as moche as for diuerses opinions had in lawe be your Justices and Barons of youre Eschequer youre lettres patentes grauntid / to youre seid besecher of vij.li.xiij.s.iiij.d. may not take effecte to the wele and profite of youre seid besecher. That it may please vnto youre hyenesse to graunte vnto youre seid besecher and to John Baret Squier youre / graciouses lettres patentes undir youre grete seal aftir the fourme contenue and effecte of a cedule to this bille annexid. And there vpon youre liberate currant and Allocate dormant in due fourme. For the whiche youre seid / besecher shall restore youre graciouses lettres patentes to hym made of vij.li.xiij.s.iiij.d. to be taken be the handes of the Abbot of Bury into the Chauncerye to be cancellid. And he shall pray to God for you.

[*On the dorse*:]

Rex apud Westmonasterium xiiijo die Nouembris anno xx. (concessit presentem billam ut petitur, et) mandavit Custodi priuati sigilli sui facere garrantum Cancellario Anglie, ut ipse desuper fieri faciat litteras patentes secundum tenorem copie presentibus annexe, presentibus Domino Suffolcie qui billam prosecutus est ac me,

Adam Moleyns

20. THE KING'S PATENT GRANTING TO LYDGATE AND BARET AND TO THE SURVIVOR THE SUM OF 7*l*.13*s*.4*d*. PER ANNUM IN LIEU OF A GRANT TO THE FORMER SURRENDERED, 21 NOVEMBER 1441. Patent Roll, 20 Henry VI, Part 1 (*CPR, Henry VI,* Vol. IV, 1441-46, p. 28): London, PRO C.66/451, m. 20. No. VIII in Steele. This grant also appears, with minor variants, in PRO SC.8/248, item 12383, following the previous item (Document 19).

Pro Johanne Lidgate Monacho et Johanne Baret Armigero.

Rex Omnibus ad quos etc. salutem. Sciatis quod cum nos septimo die Maij, Anno regni nostri decimo octauo, concesserimus Johanni Lidgate, Monacho de Bury Sancti Edmundi, septem libras tresdecim solidos et quatuor denarios, percipiendos annuatim a festo Pasche tunc vltimo preterito, durante vita sua, de exitibus et proficuis prouenientibus de alba firma et feodo vulgariter nuncupato Waytefe, per manus Abbatis de Bury Sancti Edmundi pro tempore existentis, et sic deinceps ad terminos Sancti Michaelis et Pasche per equales porciones prout in literis nostris patentibus inde sibi confectis plenius continetur. Et quia idem Johannes in voluntate existit dictas literas nostras in Cancellariam nostram ibidem restituendi cancellandas, ad intencionem quod nos sibi ac Johanni Baret Armigero septem libras tresdecim solidos et quatuor denarios percipiendos annuatim durante vita sua et alterius eorum diucius viuentis de exitibus proficuis firmis et reuencionibus Comitatuum Norffolcie et Suffolcie concedere dignaremur; Nos promissa considerantes, ac bona et gratuita seruicia que dicti Johannes et Johannes nobis impenderunt et impendent infuturum, (ac pro eo quod idem Johannes Lidgate literas predictas nobis in Cancellariam predictam restituit cancellandas), de gratia nostra speciali concessimus eisdem Johanni et Johanni, septem libras tresdecim solidos et quatuor denarios percipiendos annuatim a dicto festo Pasche durante vita sua et alterius eorum diucius viuentis, de exitibus proficuis firmis et reuencionibus Comitatuum predictorum per manus Vicecomitis eorundem Comitatuum pro tempore existentis, ad festa Pasche et Sancti Michaelis per equales porciones. In cuius etc. Teste Rege apud Westmonasterium, xxj die Nouembris.

> Per breue de priuato sigillo, et de data predicta, auctoritate Parliamenti.

21. ORDER TO THE SHERIFF OF NORFOLK AND SUFFOLK TO PAY LYDGATE AND BARET THEIR JOINT ANNUITY, 21 NOVEMBER 1441. Close Roll, 20 Henry VI (*CCR, Henry VI,* Vol. IV, 1441-47, HMSO, 1937, p. 6): London, PRO C.54/292, m. 24.

Pro Johanne Lydgate monacho

et Johanni Baret armigero [*in left margin*]

Rex Vicecomiti Norffolcie & Suffolcie qui nunc est vel qui pro tempore erit. Salutem Cum nos considerantes bona et gratuita seruicia quod Johannes Lydgate / Monachus de Bury sancti Edmundi et Johannes Baret armigerus nobis impenderunt et impendent infuturum de gratia nostra speciali concesserimus / eisdem Johanni et Johanni septem libras tresdecim solidos et quatuor denarios percipiendos annuatim a festo Pasche anno regni nostri decimo / octauo durante vita sua et alterius eorum diucius viuentis de exitibus proficuis firmis et reuencionibus Comitatuum predictorum per manus Vicecomitis eorundem / pro tempore existentis ad festa Pasche et sancti Michaelis per equales porciones prout in literis nostris patentibus inde confectis plenius continetur / tibi precipimus quod eisdem Johanni et Johanni septem libras tresdecim solidos et quatuor denarios annuos exnunc singulis annis ad / terminos predictos durante vita sua et alterius eorum diucius viuentis de exitibus proficuis firmis et reuencionibus Comitatuum predictorum soluas / iuxta tenorem literarum nostrarum predictarum Recipiens a prefatis Johanne et Johanne de tempore in tempus literas suas acquietancie que / pro nobis sufficientes fuerint in hac parte singulas soluciones quas eis sic feceritis (de tempore in tempus) testificantes per quas et presens mandatum nostrum / nos tibi inde in compoto tuo ad Scaccarium nostrum de tempore in tempus debitam allocacionem habere faciemus Teste Rege apud Westmonasterium / xxi die Nouembris

/ per breue de priuato sigillo et de data predicta auctoritate parliamenti / et erat patens

22. AN ALLOWANCE TO THE SHERIFF OF NORFOLK AND SUFFOLK OF 3*l.*16*s.*8*d.* PAID TO LYDGATE (AND BARET) FOR THE HALF-YEAR TO MICHAELMAS 1440 ON ACCOUNT OF THE GRANT OF 21 NOVEMBER 1441. Pipe Roll, 19 Henry VI (retrospective authorization in the accounting for the previous year, 18 Henry VI [i.e. 1439-40], of allowances to Miles Stapleton, Sheriff of Norfolk and Suffolk): London, PRO E.372/286, item Norff. (i.e. roll 2). No. VI in Steele.

Et Johanni Lidgate, Monacho de Bury Sancti Edmundi, et Johanni Baret Armigero, quibus Rex xxjmo die Nouembris anno xxmo concessit septem libras tresdecim solidos et quatuor denarios percipiendos annuatim a festo Pasche anno xviijuo durante vita sua et alterius eorum diucius viuentis de exitibus proficuis firmis et reuencionibus Comitatuum Norffolcie et Suffolcie prouenientibus per manus Vicecomitis eorundem Comitatuum pro tempore existentis ad festa Pasche et Sancti Michaelis per equales porciones—lxxvj.s. viij.d. de termino Sancti Michaelis anno xixno. per breue Regis irrotulatum in Memorandis de anno xxmo Regis huius, termino Sancti Michaelis. rotulo .xxxiiijto. et literas patentes ipsorum Iohannis et Iohannis de recepcione.

23. WRIT FOR PAYMENT OF ABOVE. Memoranda Rolls, 27 Henry VI: London, PRO (E.159) IND.1.7037, piece 79v.

Litere Regis patentes facte Johanni Lydgate Monacho et alijs de / quadam annuitate vij.li.xiij.s.iiij.d. percipiendorum per manus vice / comitum predictorum irrotulatum etc.

eodem Rotulo

24. ROGER CHAMBERLEYN, LATE SHERIFF OF NORFOLK AND SUFFOLK, RENDERS ACCOUNT OF PAYMENT TO MICHAELMAS 1441. Pipe Roll, 22 Henry VI (1443-44): London, PRO E.372/289, roll 4 dorse (item adhuc item Norff.). No. IX in Steele. There is an exact copy of this record in the Chancellor's Rolls, PRO E.352/235, item adhuc item Norff. dorse.

Et Johanni Lidgate Monacho de Bury sancti Edmundi et Johanni Baret armigero quibus Rex xxjmo die Nouembris anno xxmo concessit septem libras tresdecim solidos et quatuor denarios percipiendos annuatim a festo Pasche anno xviijuo durante vita sua et alterius eorum diucius viuentis de exitibus proficuis firmis et reuencionibus comitatuum Norffolcie et Suffolcie prouenientibus per manus Vicecomitis eorundem comitatuum pro tempore existentis ad festa Pasche et sancti Michaelis per equales porciones—vijli.xiijs. iiijd. de termino Pasche anno xixno et termino sancti Michaelis anno xxmo per litere Regis / irrotulato in memorandis de anno xxmo Regis huius termino sancti Trinitatis rotulo xiiimo et literas acquietancie ipsorum Johannis et Johannis de receptione.

25. WRIT FOR PAYMENT OF ABOVE. Memoranda Rolls, 20 Henry VI: London, PRO (E.159) IND.1.7037, piece 60r.

Litere Regis patentes facte Johanni Lydgate et Johanni Baret de quadam annuitate septem librarum tresdecim solidorum et quatuor denariorum percipiendorum de exitibus comitatuum Norffolcie et Suffolcie irrotulatum etc.

eodem Rotulo

Breue de Liberate Currant de quadam annuitate septem librarum tresdecim solidorum et quatuor denariorum percipiendorum per manus vicecomitis comitatuum predictorum facta Johanni Lydgate et Johanni Baret irrotulatum etc.

eodem Rotulo

26. RECORD OF PAYMENT OF ANNUITY TO MICHAELMAS 1443 BY THOMAS BREWES, SHERIFF. Pipe Roll, 21 Henry VI (1442-43): London, PRO E.372/288, roll 3 (adhuc item Norff.), halfway down. No. X in Steele. There is an exact copy of this record in the Chancellor's Rolls, PRO E.352/234, adhuc item Norff.

Et Johanni Lidgate Monacho... [as Document 24]... de termino Pasche anno / xxjmo et termino sancti Michaelis anno xxijdo per litere Regis quod est inter Communia de anno xxjmo Regis huius termino Trinitatis rotulo quinto et literas acquietancie / ipsius Johannis de recepcione.

27. RECEIPT OF BARET FOR THE HALF-YEAR'S PAYMENT, 2 OCTOBER 1446. Published by J. Zupitza in Anglia 3 (1880), 532. No. XI in Steele. (Steele searched for this payment by Sheriff William Tyrell in the Pipe Rolls for 26 to 33 Henry VI; nothing is to be found in the long Tyrell entries, of the type where reference is usually made to the payment of the annuity, in E.372/291, for 24 Henry VI. Zupitza records his find thus: "Durch das register zu Turner's katalog der urkunden der Bodleiana wurde ich auf eine Lydgate betreffende quittung vom 2. October 1446 [Suffolk, Bury St. Edmund's 121] aufmerksam, die meines wissens noch nirgends gedruckt is.")

Nouerint vniuersi per presentes me Johannem Baret armigerum recepisse pro me et Johanne Lydgate, Monacho de Bury sancti Edmundi, de Willelmo Tyrell, Vicecomite Norffolcie et Suffolcie, tres libras, sexdecim solidos et octo denarios de illis septem libris, tresdecim solidis, et quatuor denariis, quos Dominus Rex per litteras suas patentes nobis concessit percipiendos annuatim ad terminum vite nostre et alterius nostrum diucius viuentis, de exitibus, proficuis, ffirmis, et reuencionibus

Comitatuum predictorum per manus Vicecomitis eorundem, qui pro tempore fuerit, ad festa Pasche et sancti Michaelis per equales porciones, videlicet pro termino Michaelis vltimo preterito ante datum presencium. De quibus vero tribus libris, sexdecim solidis et octo denariis, pro termino Michaelis predicto fateor me pro me et predicto Johanne Lydgate esse pacatum dictumque vicecomitem inde fore quietum per presentes. In cuius rei testimonium presentibus sigillum meum apposui. Datum secundo die Octobris Anno regni Regis Henrici sexti post conquestum vicesimo quinto.

28. PAYMENT OF ANNUITY TO MICHAELMAS 1448 BY PHILIP WENTWORTH, SHERIFF. Pipe Roll, 32 Henry VI: London, PRO E.372/299, roll for City of Norwich, with Res Norff. dorse. No. XII in Steele. There is an exact copy of this record in the Chancellor's Rolls, PRO E.352/245, roll Ciuitas Norwici: Res Norff. dorse.

[*same as Document 26, E.372/288, except*] . . . de termino Pasche anno xxvito et termino sancti Michaelis anno xxvijmo Per breue . . .

29. PAYMENT OF ANNUITY TO MICHAELMAS 1449 BY GILES SEINTLO, SHERIFF. Pipe Roll, 32 Henry VI, London, PRO E.372/299, roll 3 (adhuc item Norff.), dorse. No. XIII in Steele. There is an exact copy of this record in the Chancellor's Rolls, PRO E.352/245, adhuc item Norff. dorse.

[*same as Document 26, E.372/288, except*] . . . de termino Pasche anno xxviimo et termino sancti Michaelis anno xxviiiuo per breue . . .

30. LYDGATE'S AUTOGRAPH? Oxford, Bodleian Library MS. Laud misc. 233 (Isidore, *Synonyma*; Hildebert of Le Mans, sermons; "Versus circiter cxiv proverbiales," "Versus lxxiv heroici proverbiales," etc.), f. 125v (verso of end fly-leaf). See "Life," above, note 39.

Sciant presentes et futuri quod ego Johannis Lydgate.

(Dr. Antonia Gransden is of the opinion that this is not the hand that appears in some of the annotations in a Bury copy, now Holkham MS. misc. 37 [at present in the Bodleian Library], of Guido della Colonna, *Historia destructionis Troiae*, Lydgate's direct source for his *Troy Book*. Another Bury copy of the *Historia*, now BL MS. Harley 51, has only one brief note [f. 24], not in the "Lydgate" hand.)

Manuscripts of the Major Works (by Title)

Normally, post-1600 manuscripts that are copied from prints are not listed. Folio numbers are not given where an item is the sole text in a manuscript. I am greatly indebted to Tony Edwards for his help in compiling the lists of manuscripts, and to Ian Doyle for information on dating.

COMPLAINT OF THE BLACK KNIGHT

Manuscripts briefly classified in Norton-Smith, *Lydgate: Poems* (1966), pp. 160-61; see also *IMEV* 1507, *MWME* 2085.

Cambridge, Magdalene College MS. Pepys 2006, pp. 1-17 (*c.* 1450).

Edinburgh, National Library of Scotland MS. Accession 4233 (the Asloan MS), ff. 243-46v, 293-300v (1513-30). Transcription of Chepman and Myllar print of 1508.

Edinburgh UL MS. Laing 450.

London, BL MS. Additional 16165, ff. 190v-200 (1425-50).

Oxford, Bodleian Library MS. Bodley 638, ff. 1-4v (1450-75). Lacks lines 1-467.

Oxford, Bodleian Library MS. Digby 181, ff. 31-39 (1450-1500).

Oxford, Bodleian Library MS. Fairfax 16, ff. 20v-30 (1430-50).

Oxford, Bodleian Library MS. Tanner 346, ff. 48v-59 (1430-50).

Oxford, Bodleian Library MS. Arch. Selden. B.24, ff. 120v-29v (*c.* 1486).

EXCERPT (21 stanzas) in Edinburgh, National Library of Scotland MS. 1.1.6 (the Bannatyne MS), pp. 618-21 (1568).

EARLY PRINTS by Chepman and Myllar 1508, de Worde 1531?, Thynne 1532 (and likewise in subsequent collected editions of Chaucer, with attribution to Chaucer).

DANSE MACABRE

Manuscripts described and classified in Seymour 1983; see also *IMEV* 2590, 2591, *MWME* 2088.

Cambridge, Trinity College MS. R.3.21 (601), ff. 278v-83 (1461-83).

Coventry PRO MS. 325/1, ff. 70-74v.

Leiden UL, Vossius MS. Germ. Gall.Q.9, ff. 29v-41v (1450-75).

Lincoln Cathedral Library MS. C.5.4 (129), ff. 79v-86 (c. 1450).

London, BL MS. Cotton Vespasian A.xxv, ff. 181-86 (c. 1555).

London, BL MS. Harley 116, ff. 129-40 (1450-75).

London, BL MS. Lansdowne 699, ff. 41-50 (c. 1450).

New Haven, CT, Yale UL (Beinecke) MS. 493, ff. 51v-60 (1430-60).

Oxford, Bodleian Library MS. Arch. Selden. supra 53, ff. 148-58v (c. 1430).

Oxford, Bodleian Library MS. Bodley 221, ff. 53v-61 (1430-60).

Oxford, Bodleian Library MS. Bodley 686, ff. 209-16 (1430-50).

Oxford, Bodleian Library MS. Laud 735, ff. 52v-61 (1430-60).

Oxford, Corpus Christi College MS. 237, ff. 146-57 (1450-1500).

Rome, Venerable English College MS. 1306, ff. 111v-20 (c. 1450-75). Also *Life of Our Lady*, etc.

San Marino, CA, Huntington Library MS. EL 26.A.13, ff. 1-12v (c. 1450).

EXCERPT (one stanza) in Cambridge, MA, Harvard University, Houghton Library MS. English 752 (of the *Troy Book*), f. 44 (1475-1500).

EARLY PRINTS by Fakes c. 1521 (20 stanzas only, in *Horae Beate Marie Virginis*) and Tottel 1554 (with *Fall of Princes*).

FALL OF PRINCES

Manuscripts described and briefly classified in Bergen 1927; see also *IMEV* 1168 (also 674), *MWME* 2099. For fragments and extracts, see Edwards 1971 (supplemented in *Manuscripta* 22 [1978], 176-78).

olim Audley End, Cambs. (R. H. Neville); sold at Sotheby's 8 July 1970, lot 98.

Belvoir Castle, Notts. (Duke of Rutland) MS. (1450-75).

Berkeley, CA, U. of California Library, MS. 75 (formerly Phillipps 8118, then Gribble, then Bodmer) (c. 1480).

Chicago, Newberry Library MS. 33.3 (formerly Harmsworth-Leighton, then Rosenbach 475) (1440-80).

Chicago UL MS. 565 (formerly Phillipps 4255) (1475-85). Imperfect, ends III.4769.

Glasgow UL, Hunterian MS. 5 (1450-75).

London, BL MS. Additional 21410 (*c.* 1485?).

London, BL MS. Additional 39659 (1460-70).

London, BL MS. Harley 1245 (1460-70).

London, BL MS. Harley 1766 (1450-60). An abridged version of the whole, with much variation and many additions.

London, BL MS. Harley 3486 (*c.* 1475?)

London, BL MS. Harley 4197 (1475-1500).

London, BL MS. Harley 4203 (*c.* 1470?)

London, BL MS. Royal 18 B.xxxi (1460-70).

London, BL MS. Royal 18 D.iv (*c.* 1450).

London, BL MS. Royal 18 D.v (1450-75).

London, BL MS. Sloane 4031 (*c.* 1470?).

London, Lambeth Palace Library MS. 254 (1460-70).

Longleat House, Wiltshire, MS. 254 (1460-70).

Manchester University, John Rylands Library, MS. Crawford English 2 (*c.* 1450). Copy-text for print by Pynson 1494 (see M. Morgan, in *BJRL* 33 [1950-51], 194-96).

New York, Columbia University, Plimpton MS. 225 (formerly Bourdillon) (1450-75). Very imperfect. Philadelphia Free Public Library MS. Lewis 314, a single leaf, is another part of this MS (see A. S. G. Edwards, *Manuscripta* 15 [1971], 29-31).

New York, Pierpont Morgan Library MS. 124 (formerly Lee) (1450-75).

Oxford, Bodleian Library MS. Bodley 263 (*c.* 1450). Base-MS. for Bergen's edition.

Oxford, Bodleian Library MS. e Museo 1 (*c.* 1470?). Very imperfect.

Oxford, Bodleian Library MS. Hatton 2 (formerly 105) (1480?).

Oxford, Bodleian Library MS. Rawlinson C. 448 (*c.* 1460?).

Oxford, Corpus Christi College MS. 242 (1460-70).

Philadelphia, Rosenbach Foundation MS. 439/16 (formerly Phillipps 4254) (1450-75).

Princeton UL, Garrett MS. 139 (formerly Phillipps 8117) (1450-75).

Princeton UL, Robert H. Taylor MS. (formerly Wollaton Hall) (1450-75).

San Marino, CA, Huntington Library MS. HM 268 (formerly Ecton Hall) (1445-50). Very imperfect. BL MS. Sloane 2452, ff. 1-8, is another part of this MS (see A. S. G. Edwards, *Manuscripta* 16 [1972], 37-40).

Tokyo, Takamiya MS. 40 (formerly Mostyn Hall 272, then Rosenbach 477, then Houghton 9) (1465-75?).

Urbana, IL, Illinois UL MS. 84 (1425-75). Very imperfect.

Victoria, BC, U. of Victoria, McPherson Library MS. (1450-75) (see A. S. G. Edwards, in *Manuscripta* 22 [1978], 176-78).

FRAGMENTS in Edinburgh UL MS. Laing II.514; Montreal, McGill UL MS. 143 (four non-sequential leaves) (see A. S. G. Edwards, *Scriptorium* 28 [1974], 75-77); Tokyo, Takamiya MS. 30 (formerly John E. du Pont) (8 leaves: see *TLS*, 5 May 1972, p. 522); Tregaskis Sale Catalogue 1919 (one leaf); *olim* Phillipps 23554 (Maggs sale catalogue 849, 1958, item 30A; one leaf).

EXTRACTS (Those marked with an asterisk are also listed under MINOR WORKS below.)

Cambridge UL MS. Ff. i.6* (ff. 150-51); Cambridge, Fitzwilliam Museum MS. McClean 182 (ff. 11r-v, 49v-52v); Cambridge, Magdalene College MS. Pepys 2011 (ff. 77-78); Cambridge, St. John's College MS. 223 (ff. 94-99); Cambridge, Trinity College MS. R.3.19 (599)* (ff. 2-3, 171-77, 188-202), and MS. R.3.20 (600)* (pp. 368-70); Edinburgh, National Library of Scotland MS. Advocates 1.1.6 (f. 75); Leiden University Library, Vossius MS. Germ. Gall. Q.9* (ff. 65-80, 104-06); Lismore, MS. Gaelic xxxvii (p. 184) (see R. H. Robbins, *ELN* 5 [1967], 244); London, BL MSS. Additional 29729* (ff. 169-70), Arundel 26 (f. 32), Harley 172 (ff. 1*r-v, 2-3), 367* (ff. 83-86) (see Edwards, *NQ* [1969], 171), 2202 (ff. 71-2v), 2251* (ff. 81v-145v), 2255* (ff. 94v-96v), 4011 (ff. 1v-2v), Lansdowne 699* (ff. 51-66, 91-94); New York, Pierpont Morgan Library MS. M4 (ff. 74-75); Oxford, Bodleian Library MSS. Arch.Selden B.10* (ff. 200-05, copy of de Worde print), Ashmole 59* (ff. 13-17v, 28-29v, 59, 183), Digby 181* (ff. 8-10, 52-53); Oxford, Balliol College MS. 329* (ff. 127-71).

See also London, BL MS. Harley 1706 (f. 19) = *IMEV* 2585; Cambridge UL MS. Ff.v.45 (f. 13) and Oxford, Bodleian Library MS.Douce 322 (ff. 19-20) = *IMEV* 3143.

EARLY PRINTS Richard Pynson (1494 and 1527), Richard Tottel (1554) and John Wayland (1554?). Wynkyn de Worde printed in

1510(?) and 1520(?) extracts from the *Fall*, with other short poems by Lydgate and Chaucer, and called them "The prouerbes of Lydgate."

LIFE OF OUR LADY

Manuscripts described and classified in Lauritis 1961; see also *IMEV* 2574, *MWME* 2128.

Aberystwyth, National Library of Wales MS. 21242C (formerly Mostyn Hall 85, sold at Christie's 24 October 1974, lot 1480) (*c.* 1450).

Cambridge, Trinity College MS. R.3.21 (601), ff. 85-156 (1461-83).

Cambridge, Trinity College MS. R.3.22 (602), ff. 1-110 (1425-50). Also Hoccleve's *Regement.*

Cambridge UL MS. Additional 3303(7), ff. 1-4 (portions from Book III). Columbia, MO, University of Missouri Library MS. (*Fragmenta Manuscripta*), f. 178 (V.344-64, 372-92), is part of this same MS. (see A. S. G. Edwards and A. W. Jenkins, in *ELN* 9 [1971], 1-3; also H. G. Jones, in *ELN* 7 [1969], 93-96).

Cambridge UL MS. Kk.1.3 (part 10), ff. 2-94 (1425-50). Also Hoccleve's *Regement*; *Prioress's Tale*, etc.

Cambridge UL MS. Mm. vi.5 (1425-50).

Chicago, U. of Chicago Library MS. 566 ff. 4-107v (1450-1500).

Durham, UL MS. Cosin V.ii.16 (1425-50). Base-MS for Lauritis 1961.

Edinburgh, National Library of Scotland, Advocates MS. 19.3.1, ff. 176-210 (1450-1500). Books IV-VI only.

Glasgow UL, Hunterian MS. 232 (1450-1500).

Liverpool Cathedral Library, MS. Radcliffe 16 (*c.* 1600). Copy of Caxton 1484.

London, BL MS. Additional 19252 (1425-50).

London, BL MS. Additional 19452 (1425-50).

London, BL MS. Arundel 168, ff. 66-88 (1450-1500). Fragment (I.414-III.1208).

London, BL MS. Cotton Appendix VIII (1450-1500).

London, BL MS. Harley 629 (1450-1500).

London, BL MS. Harley 1304, ff. 4-99 (1450-1500).

London, BL MS. Harley 2382, ff. 1-74 (1470-1500). Mixed affiliation. Also *Testament*; *Prioress's Tale, Second Nun's Tale.* (London, BL MS. Sloane 297, f. 88, is a leaf torn from this MS.)

London, BL MS. Harley 3862 (1450-1500).

London, BL MS. Harley 3952 (1450-1500).

London, BL MS. Harley 4011, ff. 23-119 (1450-1500). A few other short poems by Lydgate.

London, BL MS. Harley 4260 (1450-1500).

London, BL MS. Harley 5272 (1450-1500).

London, BL MS. Sloane 1785, ff. 14-29 (1450-1500). A fragment (I.434-795).

London, Lambeth Palace Library MS. 344, ff. 14v-99 (1450-1500). A few other short poems by Lydgate.

London, Society of Antiquaries MS. 134, ff. 1-30 (1425-50). Also Gower's *Confessio*, Hoccleve's *Regement*, Walton's Boethius.

Longleat House, Wiltshire, MS. 15 (1450-1500).

Manchester, Chetham Library MS. 6709, ff. 6-156 (1490, copy of Caxton 1484). Also *St. Edmund, St. George, St. Margaret*, etc.; see below.

New Haven, CT, Yale UL (Beinecke) MS. 281, ff. 4-114v.

New Haven, CT, Yale UL (Beinecke) MS. 660, ff. 1-76v (formerly Marquess of Bute; sold Sotheby's sale 13 June 1983, lot 9).

Oxford, Bodleian Library MS. Ashmole 39 (1450-1500).

Oxford, Bodleian Library MS. Ashmole 59 (part 2), ff. 135-81 (*c.* 1500, with later hand, *c.* 1600, supplying beginning, ff. 135-43). Other Lydgate contents in part 1; see below.

Oxford, Bodleian Library MS. Bodley 75 (1475-1500).

Oxford, Bodleian Library MS. Bodley 120 (1450-1500).

Oxford, Bodleian Library MS. Bodley 596(B), ff. 86-174 (1450-1500).

Oxford, Bodleian Library MS. Hatton 73, ff. 10-118 (*c.* 1450). Other minor poems by Lydgate.

Oxford, Bodleian Library MS. Rawlinson poet. F. 140 (1450-1500).

Oxford, Corpus Christi College MS. 237, ff. 157-240 (1450-1500). Also *Danse Macabre*, etc.

Oxford, St. John's College MS. 56, ff. 1-74 (1450-1500). Mixed affiliation. Other minor poems by Lydgate.

Rome, Venerable English College MS. 1306 (also numbered 127 or A.347), ff. 1-65 (1450-1475). Imperfect (begins II.365). Also *Danse Macabre*, etc. See R. A. Klinefelter, in *MLQ* 14 (1953), 3-6.

San Marino, CA, Huntington Library MS. HM 115, ff 2v-112 (1425-50).

San Marino, CA, Huntington Library MS. HM 144, ff. 11-20 (1480-1500). II.1-504 only. Other Lydgate contents; see below.

Urbana, IL, Illinois UL MS. 85, ff. 2-83v (formerly Mostyn Hall 257, sold at Sotheby's in 1920 to Leicester Harmsworth and in 1948 to Stonehill).

EXTRACT in Dublin, Trinity College MS. 423 (D.4.3), f. 102v (1475-1525) (III.1-7) (see R. H. Robbins, in *ELN* 5 [1968], 243-47). *Magnificat* (II.981-1060) in Cambridge, Gonville and Caius College MS. 230, ff. 54-55 (1450-1500); Edinburgh, National Library of Scotland, Advocates MS. 1.1.6 (the Bannatyne MS.), ff. 25-6 (1568); London, BL MS. Additional 29729, ff. 122-23 (1558).

EARLY PRINTS by Caxton 1484, Redman 1531.

PILGRIMAGE OF THE LIFE OF MAN

Manuscripts described in Furnivall and Locock 1899; see also *IMEV* 4265, *MWME* 2143.

London, BL MS. Cotton Tiberius A.vii, ff. 39-106 (1430-50). Fragmentary (lines 18313-23676 only).

London, BL MS. Cotton Vitellius C.xiii (1450-1500).

London, BL MS. Stowe 952 (1450-1500 to f. 304, line 17197; remainder copied in by Stow, 1575-1600).

Worcester Cathedral Library MS. C.i.8. Fragment on a pastedown.

EARLY PRINT by Caxton 1483.

ST. ALBON AND ST. AMPHIBALUS

Manuscripts described and classified by Van der Westhuizen 1974 and Reinecke 1985; see also *IMEV* 3748, *MWME* 2077.

Lincoln, Cathedral Library MS. C.5.4 (129), ff. 1-89 (*c.* 1450). Other Lydgate contents; see below.

London, BL MS. Lansdowne 699, ff. 96-176 (*c.* 1450). Base-MS for Van der Westhuizen 1974 and Reinecke 1985. Other Lydgate contents; see below.

London, Inner Temple Library, Petyt MS. 511, part xi (1450-75).

Oxford, Trinity College MS. 38, ff. 1-67 (1450-1500).

San Marino, CA, Huntington Library MS. HM 140 (formerly Phillipps 8299), ff. 1-66 (1475-1500). A few short pieces by Lydgate; also *Clerk's Tale.*

EXTRACT in Cambridge, Fitzwilliam Museum MS. McClean 40-1950 (the "Talbot Hours"), f. 135v (1450-75). III.1499-1526 (prayer to St. Albon).

EARLY PRINT by John Herford, St. Albans, 1534.

ST. EDMUND AND ST. FREMUND

Manuscripts described and classified in Seymour 1983; see also *IMEV* 3440, *MWME* 2096.

Arundel Castle, Sussex (Duke of Norfolk) MS. (1460-70).

Cambridge UL MS. Ee.ii.15 (part 2), ff. 48-105 (*c.* 1470).

London, BL MS. Harley 372, ff. 1-43 (1450-60). Other Lydgate contents; see below.

London, BL MS. Harley 2278 (*c.* 1435?). Base-MS. for editions of Horstmann and Miller.

London, BL MS. Harley 4826, ff. 4-45v (1460-70). Also *Secrees*; Hoccleve's *Regement of Princes.*

London, BL MS. Harley 7333, ff. 136-47v (1450-60). Other Lydgate contents; see below.

London, BL Yates Thompson MS. 47 (1460-70) (formerly Mostyn Hall 84).

Manchester, Chetham Library MS. 6709, ff. 199-282v (1490). Also *Life of Our Lady* and other Lydgate contents; see below.

Oxford, Bodleian Library MS. Ashmole 46, ff. 1-96 (1460-70). Also *Secrees.*

Oxford, Bodleian Library MS. Rawlinson B.216, ff. 162v-71 (1450-75). Very imperfect (I.81-II.294 only).

Oxford, Bodleian Library MS. Tanner 347 (1460-70).

Oxford, Corpus Christi College MS. 61 (1450-75).

EXTRACTS in London, BL MS. Harley 247, f. 45 (prose paraphrase of extracts from first half of poem in hand of John Stow, *c.* 1600), and Harley 367, f. 86 (III.1457-1562, in hand of John Stow); Bodleian Library MS. Ashmole 59, ff. 22-24 (III.1457-1562).

FRAGMENT in Exeter, City Record Office, Misc. Roll 59 (bifolium, containing I.1032-II.14).

SECREES OF OLD PHILISOFFRES

Manuscripts described in *Secrees*, ed. Steele 1894 (London MSS. only); see also *IMEV* 935, *MWME* 2152.

Cambridge, Fitzwilliam Museum MS. McClean 182, ff. 12-49 (*c.* 1450). Also *Serpent of Division.*

Cambridge, Fitzwilliam Museum MS. McClean 183, ff. 1-47 + a single leaf, BL MS. Additional 39922, f. 16.

Cambridge, Gonville & Caius College MS. 336, ff. 104-24.

Cambridge, Trinity College MS. O.3.40 (1212), ff. 1-44.

London, BL MS. Additional 14408, ff. 1-48v (1473).

London, BL MS. Additional 34360, ff. 78-116 (1461-83). An important Lydgate manuscript; see below.

London, BL MS. Additional 60577, ff. 24v-37v.

London, BL MS. Arundel 59, ff. 90-130 (*c.* 1470). Also Hoccleve's *Regement.*

London, BL MS. Harley 2251, ff. 188v-224 (1464-83).

London, BL MS. Harley 4826, ff. 52-81 (1460-70). Also *St. Edmund;* Hoccleve's *Regement.*

London, BL MS. Lansdowne 285, ff. 152-99v (1460-70). Sir John Paston's "Grete Booke."

London, BL MS. Sloane 2027, ff. 53-92v (1450-75).

London, BL MS. Sloane 2464, ff. 1-65 (1450-75). Base-MS. for Steele's edition.

New York, Pierpont Morgan Library MS. M775, ff. 139-95 (*c.* 1486).

Oxford, Bodleian Library MS. Ashmole 46, ff. 97-160 (1460-70). Also *St. Edmund.*

Oxford, Bodleian Library MS. Laud misc. 416, ff. 255-87 (1459).

Oxford, Bodleian Library MS Laud misc. 673, ff. 1-73.

Oxford, Balliol College MS. 329, ff. 80-126 (1450-1500). Other Lydgate contents; see below.

MS. sold at Christie's, 8 November, 1978, lot. 198, ff. 1-19v.

EXTRACTS in Cambridge, Gonville and Caius College MS. 336, ff. 104-24, and Trinity College MS. R.3.19, ff. 49-52.

FRAGMENT in Philadelphia Free Public Library MS. Lewis 304 (single leaf fragment)

EARLY PRINTS by Pynson 1511, 1527.

SERPENT OF DIVISION

Manuscripts described and classified in MacCracken 1911; see also *MWME* 2154; *Index of Printed Middle English Prose*, ed. R. E. Lewis, N. F. Blake, A. S. G. Edwards (New York and London 1985), p. 281.

Cambridge, Fitzwilliam Museum MS. McClean 182, ff. 1-10 (*c.* 1450). Also *Secrees*; Hoccleve's *Regement*. Base-MS. for most of MacCracken 1911.

Cambridge, Magdalene College MS. Pepys 2006, pp. 191-209 (*c.* 1450).

Cambridge, MA, Harvard University, Houghton Library MS. English 530 (formerly A.R.5), ff. 49-57 (1440-64). Also prose *Brut*, etc. See Robinson 1899.

London, BL MS. Additional 48031 (formerly Baron Calthorpe, Yelverton MS. 35), ff. 165-75 (*c.* 1460?). Base-MS. for part of MacCracken 1911.

EARLY PRINTS by P. Treverys (1521-35?), R. Redman (*c.* 1535), Owen Rogers 1559, E. Allde 1590.

SIEGE OF THEBES

Manuscripts described and classified in Erdmann and Ekwall 1930; see also *IMEV* 3928, *MWME* 2155.

Austin, TX, U. of Texas Library MS. 143 (formerly Deene Park), ff. 246-304 (1425-75). Also *Churl and Bird*.

Boston Public Library MS. F. med.94 (formerly Bristol, Newton Park, Temple MS., Sotheby's sale 16 June 1941, lot 153), ff. 1-76 (1420-40). See A. S. G. Edwards, in *Yale UL Gazette*, Supplement 66 (1991), 181-86.

Cambridge, Magdalene College MS Pepys 2011, ff. 1-76 (1450-1500). Also *Letter to Gloucester*.

Cambridge, Trinity College MS. O.5.2 (1283), ff. 191-211v (1450-1500). Also *Troy*; *Generydes*.

Cambridge, Trinity College MS. R.4.20 (652), ff. 89-169 (*c.* 1440).

Cambridge UL MS. Add. 3137, ff. 1-48 (1450-1500).

Cambridge UL MS. Add. 6864, ff. 1-75 (formerly Gurney) (1450-1500).

Coventry City Record Office MS. 325/1, ff. 137-67v (1440-75). Also *Danse Macabre*; Hoccleve's *Regement*, etc. (see A. I. Doyle and G. Pace, in *PMLA* 83 [1968], 22-34).

Durham UL MS. Cosin V.ii.14, ff. 1-68v (*c.* 1450) Also *St. Margaret.*

London, BL MS. Additional 5140, ff. 358-423v (1475-1500). Also *Canterbury Tales.*

London, BL MS Additional 18632, ff. 5-33 (*c.* 1440). Also Hoccleve's *Regement.*

London, BL MS Additional 29729, ff. 17-83 (1558). Much else by Lydgate; see below.

London, BL MS. Arundel 119, ff. 1-80 (1425-30). Base-MS for Erdmann and Ekwall 1930.

London, BL MS. Cotton Appendix XXVII, ff. 1-51 (1500-1600).

London, BL MS. Egerton 2864 (formerly Ingilby), ff. 301v-350 (1460-80). Also *Canterbury Tales.*

London, BL MS. Royal 18 D.ii, ff. 147v-62 (*c.* 1460). Also *Troy, Testament.*

London, Lambeth Palace Library MS. 742, ff. 1-68v (*c.* 1450).

Longleat House, Wiltshire, MS. 257, ff. 1-48 (1450-70).

New Haven, Yale University, Beinecke Library MS. 661, ff. 1-61 (formerly Mostyn Hall 258) (1450-1500).

New York, Pierpont Morgan Library MS. 4, ff. 1-74 (*c.* 1450). Also *Letter to Gloucester*, etc. (see C. F. Buhler, in *MLN* 52 [1937], 1-9).

Old Buckenham Hall, Norfolk, Prince Duleep Singh's MS. (1475-1500). Untraced.

Oxford, Bodleian Library MS. Bodley 776 (1430-40).

Oxford, Bodleian Library MS. Digby 230, ff. 1-27v (1420-35). Also *Troy.*

Oxford, Bodleian Library MS. Laud misc.416, ff. 227-54 (1459). Also *Secrees*, etc.

Oxford, Bodleian Library MS. Laud misc.557, ff. 1-66 (1450-1500).

Oxford, Bodleian Library MS. Rawlinson c.48, ff. 5-78) (*c.* 1450). Other Lydgate contents; see below.

Oxford, Christ Church MS. 152, ff. 291-350 (1460-1500). Also *Churl and Bird*. A *Canterbury Tales* MS.

Oxford, St. John's College MS. 256 (*c.* 1476). Copy-text for print by De Worde (see G. Bone, in *Library*, 4th series, 12 [1932], 284-306).

olim Temple. Sotheby's sale 6 November 1899, lot 408. Untraced.

FRAGMENT in Cambridge, UL MS. Additional 2707 (2)(BB), f. 1 (fragmentary first leaf of a copy of the poem: see A. S. G. Edwards, in *NM* 71 [1970], 133-36).

EARLY PRINTS Wynkyn de Worde (1497?). In the 1561 reprint of Thynne's 1532 edition of the collected works of Chaucer, with additions by John Stow, and in subsequent editions of Chaucer in 1598, 1602, etc. (by virtue of its fictional claim to be a "Canterbury Tale").

TEMPLE OF GLASS

Manuscripts briefly classified in Norton-Smith, *Lydgate: Poems* (1966), p. 176, and Seymour 1983, pp. 23-24; see also *IMEV* 851, *MWME* 2160.

Cambridge, Magdalene College MS. Pepys 2006, pp. 17-52 (*c.* 1450).

Cambridge UL MS. Gg.4.27(1), ff. 490v-509v (1420-30). A large Chaucer collection.

London, BL MS. Additional 16165, ff. 206v-41 (1425-50).

Longleat House, Wiltshire, MS. 258, ff. 1-32 (1460-70).

Oxford, Bodleian Library MS. Bodley 638, ff. 16v-38 (1450-75).

Oxford, Bodleian Library MS. Fairfax 16, ff. 63-82v (1430-50).

Oxford, Bodleian Library MS. Tanner 346, ff. 76-97 (1430-50).

FRAGMENTS in London, BL MS. Sloane 1212, ff. 1, 2 (lines 736-54), 2 (lines 98-162) and 4 (part of *Compleynt*).

EARLY PRINTS by Caxton ?1477, de Worde ?1495, ?1500, ?1506, Pynson 1503, Berthelet ?1529.

TROY BOOK

Manuscripts described and partly classified in Bergen 1935; see also *IMEV* 2516, *MWME* 2168.

Bristol, City Reference Library MS. 8, ff. 1-120v (1420-35).

Cambridge, Trinity College MS. O.5.2 (1283), ff. 38-190 (1440-50). Also *Thebes*; *Generydes*.

Cambridge UL MS. Kk.v.30, ff. 19-304v (1500-25).

Cambridge, MA, Harvard University, Houghton Library MS. English 752, ff. 1-362v (formerly Ashburnham 131, formerly Harvard *27282.67.10) (*c.* 1490).

Geneva, Switzerland, Fondation Martin Bodmer cod. 110, ff. 1-365v (formerly Phillipps 3113) (*c.* 1500).

Gloucester Cathedral Library MS. 5, ff. 1-372v (*c.* 1470).

London, BL MS. Arundel 99 (1430-50).

London, BL MS. Cotton Augustus A.iv, ff. 1-155 (1420-30). Base-MS. of Bergen's edition.

London, BL MS. Royal 18.D.ii (part 1), ff. 6-146 (1450-60). Also *Testament, Thebes.*

London, BL MS. Royal 18.D.vi, ff. 4-139v (*c.* 1480).

Manchester University, John Rylands Library MS. English 1 (1440-60).

New York, Pierpont Morgan Library MS. M876 (formerly Helmingham Hall), ff. 1-102v (1435-50). Also *Sir Generides.*

Oxford, Bodleian Library MS. Digby 230, ff. 28-194v (1420-35). Also *Thebes.*

Oxford, Bodleian Library MS. Digby 232, ff. 1-157 (1420-35).

Oxford, Bodleian Library MS. Douce 148, ff. 1-289v, 301-306 (1500-25). Imperfect.

Oxford, Bodleian Library MS. Rawlinson C.446, ff. 1-404 (1420-35).

Oxford, Bodleian Library MS. Rawlinson poet. F. 144, ff. i-x (fragment) (*c.* 1500).

Oxford, Christ Church MS. 153, ff. 1-107v.

Oxford, Exeter College MS. 129, ff. 1-139 (*c.* 1480).

Oxford, St. John's College MS. 6, ff. 1-134 (1450-75).

FRAGMENTS in London, Inner Temple MS. 524 (on a flyleaf); Oxford, Bodleian Library MS. Rawlinson D.913, ff. 2-3; Oxford, Bodleian Library MS. Rawlinson poet. F. 223, ff. 3-12.

EXTRACT (= *IMEV* 1164) in London, BL MS. Royal 18 C. II, f. 1 (II.1849-56) (see A. S. G. Edwards in *NQ* 234 [1989], 307-8).

EARLY PRINTS By Richard Pynson (1513), Marshe (1555); a modernised version by Thomas Heywood (1614) in 6-line stanzas.

Manuscripts of Other Works by Lydgate

For a full listing of manuscripts, poem by poem, see *MWME*. The following listing is selective, and does not normally take account of manuscripts containing only such poems as the *Dietary, Stans puer ad mensam,* or the *Verses on the Kings of England,* nor of manuscripts containing only a single short or fragmentary Lydgate text. In the description of the contents of a manuscript, "etc." means "a few shorter pieces."

Boston Public Library MS. F.med.92 (c. 1470). *Churl and Bird*. Sotheby sale 31 March 1936, lot 146.

Cambridge UL MS. Ff.i.6 (1450-75). The "Findern anthology." A few short pieces by Lydgate.

Cambridge UL MS. Hh.iv.12 (1475-1500). *Churl and Bird, Fabula duorum mercatorum, Horns Away, Horse, Goose and Sheep*, etc.

Cambridge UL MS. Kk.i.6 (1450-1500). *Churl and Bird*, etc.

Cambridge University Library MS. Ll.v.18 (1450-1500). *St. Margaret*.

Cambridge, Jesus College MS. 56 (1450-1500). *Horns Away, Testament*, and 20 short didactic and religious pieces.

Cambridge, Magdalene College MS. Pepys 2006 (c. 1450). A large Chaucerian anthology. *Black Knight, Serpent of Division, Temple of Glass*, etc.

Cambridge, Sidney Sussex College MS. 37 (1425-50). A few short prayers.

Cambridge, Trinity College MS. R.3.19 (599) (c. 1500). A large miscellany. *Bycorne and Chichevache, Churl and Bird, Horns Away, Isopes Fabules, Secrees, Testament*, etc.

Cambridge, Trinity College MS. R.3.20 (600) (1425-50). Copied by Shirley. *Bycorne and Chichevache, Life of St. George*, six Mummings, *St. Margaret, Saying of the Nightingale*, and many shorter pieces.

Cambridge, Trinity College MS. R.3.21 (601) (1461-83). *Guy of Warwick, St. George*, etc. Also *Danse Macabre, Life of Our Lady*.

Cambridge, MA, Harvard University, Houghton Library MS. English 530 (1440-64). A *Brut* MS. *Guy of Warwick, Serpent of Division*.

Dublin, Trinity College MS. 516 (1440-45). *Dietary, Kings of England*.

Leiden UL, Vossius MS. Germ.Gall.Q.9 (1450-75). *Churl and Bird, Danse Macabre, Fabula duorum mercatorum, Guy of Warwick, Horns Away, Horse, Goose and Sheep, Letter to Gloucester, Testament*, and many other pieces. An important Lydgate MS. Related to BL MS. Lansdowne 699. See J. A. van Dorsten, *Scriptorium* 14 (1960), 315-25.

Lincoln Cathedral Library MS. C.5.4 (129) (c. 1450). *Churl and Bird, St. Austin at Compton*. Also *Danse Macabre, St. Albon*.

London, BL MS. Additional 16165 (1425-50). Copied by John Shirley. *Black Knight, Departing of Thomas Chaucer* (unique copy), *Temple of Glass*, etc.

London, BL MS. Additional 29729 (1558). Copied by John Stow from Trinity R.3.20 and other MSS. *Bycorne and Chichevache, Reason and Sensuality* (from Fairfax 16), *St. Margaret, Saying of the Nightingale, Testament*, six Mummings, many shorter pieces. Also *Thebes*.

London, BL MS. Additional 31042 (1425-50). Copied by Robert Thornton. A few short pieces.

London, BL MS. Additional 34193 (1450-1500). *Testament.*

London, BL MS. Additional 34360 (1461-83). Derived from a lost Shirley MS (cf. Harley 2251). *Fabula duorum mercatorum, Horns Away, Horse, Goose and Sheep, Letter to Gloucester, Secrees,* many shorter pieces.

London, BL MS. Cotton Caligula A.ii (1400-50). Large romance miscellany. *Churl and Bird*, etc.

London, BL MS. Harley 116 (1450-75). *Churl and Bird, Danse Macabre,* etc.

London, BL MS. Harley 218 (1450-1500). *Testament.*

London, BL MS. Harley 367 (1600-25). *St. Margaret,* etc.

London, BL MS. Harley 372 (*c.* 1450). A few short pieces.

London, BL MS. Harley 2251 (1464-83). Derived from a lost Shirley MS (cf. BL Add.34360). *Bycorne and Chichevache, Fabula duorum mercatorum, Horns Away, Horse, Goose and Sheep, Isopes Fabules, Letter to Gloucester, Saying of the Nightingale, Secrees, Testament,* many other of the shorter non-courtly poems. A major Lydgate "anthology."

London, BL MS. Harley 2255 (1440-50). *Fabula duorum mercatorum, Horns Away, Letter to Gloucester, Testament,* many other poems, chiefly religious. Done for abbot Curteys, perhaps at Bury. A major Lydgate "anthology."

London, BL MS. Harley 2407 (1450-1500). *Churl and Bird* (in a collection on alchemy and magic).

London, BL MS. Harley 7333 (*c.* 1450). A *Canterbury Tales* MS, in part descended from a lost Shirley MS. *Guy of Warwick, Title and Pedigree* (unique copy), etc. Also *St. Edmund.*

London, BL MS. Harley 7578 (*c.* 1450). A few short pieces.

London, BL MS. Lansdowne 699 (*c.* 1450). *Churl and Bird, Fabula duorum mercatorum, Guy of Warwick, Horse, Goose and Sheep, Letter to Gloucester,* and eleven other pieces. Also *Danse Macabre, St. Albon.* An important Lydgate MS.

London, Lambeth Palace Library MS. 306 (1475-1500). Large miscellany. *Horse, Goose and Sheep.*

London, Lambeth Palace Library MS. 853 (*c.* 1430). A few short pieces.

Longleat House, Wiltshire, MS. 258 (1450-75). *Churl and Bird, Temple of Glass.*

Manchester, Chetham Library MS. 6709 (1490). *St. George, St. Margaret,* etc. Also *Life of Our Lady, St. Edmund; Prioress's Tale, Second Nun's Tale.*

Oxford, Bodleian Library MS. Arch. Selden B.10 (*c.* 1470-80). A few minor pieces.

Oxford, Bodleian Library MS. Arch. Selden B.24 (*c.* 1486). A "courtly" anthology. *Black Knight.*

Oxford, Bodleian Library MS. Ashmole 59, part 1 (*c.* 1450). Copied by John Shirley. *Horns Away, Isopes Fabules, Mumming at Bishopswood* (unique copy), many shorter pieces. Also *Life of Our Lady* (in part 2, in a later hand).

Oxford, Bodleian Library MS. Ashmole 754 (1450-1500). *Horse, Goose and Sheep.*

Oxford, Bodleian Library MS. Bodley 638 (1450-75). Anthology of Chaucerian courtly poems. *Black Knight, Temple of Glass.*

Oxford, Bodleian Library MS. Bodley 686 (1430-50). A *Canterbury Tales* MS. *Danse Macabre, St. George, St. Margaret,* etc.

Oxford, Bodleian Library MS. Digby 181 (1450-1500). Anthology of Chaucerian courtly poems. *Black Knight,* etc.

Oxford, Bodleian Library MS. Fairfax 16 (1430-50). The most important of the "Hammond group" of MSS of Chaucerian courtly poems. *Black Knight, Reason and Sensuality, Temple of Glass,* etc.

Oxford, Bodleian Library MS. Laud misc. 598 (1450-1500). *Horse, Goose and Sheep,* etc.

Oxford, Bodleian Library MS. Laud misc. 673 (1450-1500). *Secrees,* etc.

Oxford, Bodleian Library MS. Laud misc. 683 (1450-1500). *Guy of Warwick, Horns Away, Testament,* and some 20 other poems, mostly prayers and hymns.

Oxford, Bodleian Library MS. Rawlinson C.48 (*c.* 1450). *Horse, Goose and Sheep,* a few short satirical and didactic poems. Also *Thebes.*

Oxford, Bodleian Library MS. Rawlinson C.86 (1450-75). *Horns Away, Horse, Goose and Sheep, Testament,* and several shorter pieces.

Oxford, Bodleian Library MS. Rawlinson poet. F.32 (1450-1500). *Fabula duorum mercatorum,* etc.

Oxford, Bodleian Library MS. Tanner 346 (1430-50). Anthology of Chaucerian courtly poems. *Black Knight, Temple of Glass.*

Oxford, Balliol College MS. 329 (1450-1500). *Secrees*, etc.

Oxford, Balliol College MS. 354 (1518-36). Richard Hill's miscellany. *Churl and Bird, Virtues of the Mass*, etc.

San Marino, CA, Huntington Library MS. EL 26.A.13 (*c.* 1450). *Danse Macabre*, etc. Hoccleve's *Regement of Princes*.

San Marino, CA, Huntington Library MS. HM 144 (1475-1500). *Churl and Bird, Horse, Goose and Sheep*, etc.

EARLY PRINTS of *Churl and Bird* (Caxton ?1477, ?1478, Pynson 1493, ?1497. de Worde ?1510, Mychel ?1550, Copland ?1565), *Horse, Goose and Sheep* (Caxton ?1477, ?1478, de Worde 1500), *Testament* (Pynson ?1520).

Modern Editions

The Dance of Death, ed. F. Warren and B. White, EETS o.s. 181 (1931). Also in Hammond 1927, below.

The Fall of Princes, ed. H. Bergen, in 4 Parts, EETS e.s. 121-24 (1924-27).

The Life of Our Lady, ed. J. A. Lauritis, R. A. Klinefelter and V. F. Gallagher, Duquesne Studies, Philological Series 2 (Pittsburgh 1961).

Minor Poems, ed. H. N. MacCracken, in 2 Parts (Part 1, Religious Poems, with an Essay on the Lydgate Canon; Part 2, Secular Poems), EETS e.s. 107, 192 (1911-34).

The Pilgrimage of the Life of Man, ed. F. J. Furnivall and K. B. Locock, in 3 Parts, EETS e.s. 77, 83, 92 (1899-1904).

Reson and Sensuallyte, ed. E. Sieper, in 2 Parts, EETS e.s. 84, 89 (1901-03).

Saint Albon and Saint Amphibalus, ed. G. Reinecke, Garland Medieval Texts, No. 11 (New York 1985); earlier edn. by J. E. Van der Westhuizen, *The Life of Saint Alban and Saint Amphibal* (Leiden 1974).

Saint Edmund and Saint Fremund, ed. J. I. Miller, Ph.D. diss. (unpublished), Harvard University (1967); earlier edn. by C. Horstmann in *Altenglische Legenden: neue Folge* (Heilbronn 1881).

Secrees of old Philisoffres, ed. R. Steele, EETS e.s. 66 (1894).

The Serpent of Division, ed. H. N. MacCracken (London and New Haven 1911).

The Siege of Thebes, ed. A. Erdmann and E. Ekwall, in 2 Parts, EETS e.s. 108, 125 (1911-30).

The Temple of Glas, ed. J. Schick, EETS e.s. 60 (1891). Also in Norton-Smith 1966, below.

Troy Book, ed. H. Bergen, in 4 Parts, EETS e.s. 97, 103, 106, 126 (1906-1935).

SELECTIONS

Norton-Smith, J., ed., *John Lydgate: Poems*, Clarendon Medieval and Tudor Series (Oxford 1966).

Hammond, E. P., ed., *English Verse between Chaucer and Surrey* (Durham, North Carolina, 1927).

Secondary Sources

For a detailed Lydgate bibliography (to 1980), see *MWME*; for documents relating to Bury, see Thomson 1980. Works relating to Lydgate found in *MWME* are selectively listed here for the period to 1975, with concentration on those relevant to the events of his life; works of more recent years are more fully represented.

Allen, R. S., "*The Siege of Thebes*: Lydgate's Canterbury Tale," in *Chaucer and Fifteenth-Century Poetry*, London Medieval Studies 5 (King's College London 1991), 122-42.

Allmand, C., *Henry V* (London 1992).

Arnold, T., ed., *Memorials of St. Edmund's Abbey*, 3 vols. Rolls Series 96 (London 1896).

Ayers, R. W., "Medieval History, Moral Purpose, and the Structure of Lydgate's *Siege of Thebes*," PMLA 73 (1958), 463-74.

Bennett, H. S., *Chaucer and the Fifteenth Century* (Oxford 1947), 137-46.

Benson, C. D., *The History of Troy in Middle English Literature* (Woodbridge 1980), 97-129.

———. "Critic and Poet: What Lydgate and Henryson did to Chaucer's *Troilus and Criseyde*," MLQ 53 (1992), 23-40.

Blake, N. F., "John Lydgate and William Caxton," *Leeds Studies in English,* n.s. 16 (1985), 272-89.

Boffey, J., *Manuscripts of English Courtly Love Lyrics in the Later Middle Ages* (Woodbridge 1985).

———. "Lydgate, Henryson, and the Literary Testament," *MLQ* 53 (1992), 41-56.

Bowers, J. M., "*The Tale of Beryn* and *The Siege of Thebes*: Alternative Ideas of *the Canterbury Tales,*" *Studies in the Age of Chaucer* 7 (1985), 23-50.

———. "*Mankind* and the Political Interests of Bury St. Edmunds," *Aestel* 2 (1994), 77-103.

Brie, F., "Mittelalter und Antike bei Lydgate," *Englische Studien* 64 (1929), 261-301.

Brusendorff, A., *The Chaucer Tradition* (Oxford 1925).

Clogan, P. M., "Lydgate and the *Roman Antique,*" *Florilegium* 11 (1992), 7-21.

Copeland, R. M., "Lydgate, Hawes, and the Science of Rhetoric in the Late Middle Ages," *MLQ* 53 (1992), 57-82.

Cornell, C., "'Purtreture' and 'Holsom Stories': John Lydgate's Accommodation of Image and Text in Three Religious Lyrics,'" *Florilegium* 10 (1988-91), 167-78.

Davidoff, J. M., "The Audience Illuminated, or New Light Shed on the Dream Frame of Lydgate's *Temple of Glas,*" *Studies in the Age of Chaucer* 5 (1983), 103-25.

Devon, F., *Issues of the Exchequer, Henry III to Henry VI* (London 1837).

Doyle, A. I., "More Light on John Shirley," *Medium Aevum* 30 (1961), 93-101.

———. "English Books In and Out of Court," in *English Court Culture in the Later Middle Ages,* ed. V. J. Scattergood and J. W. Sherborne (London 1983), 163-81.

Dugdale, Sir William, *Monasticon Anglicanum,* 6 vols. (London 1846), III.98-176 (Bury St. Edmunds).

Dwyer, R. A., "Arthur's Stellification in the *Fall of Princes,*" *Philological Quarterly* 57 (1978), 155-71.

Ebin, L. A., "Lydgate's Views on Poetry," *Annuale Mediaevale* 18 (1977), 76-105.

———. "Chaucer, Lydgate, and the 'Myrie Tale,'" *Chaucer Review* 13 (1978-79), 316-36.

————. *John Lydgate*, Twayne's English Authors Series 407 (Boston 1985).

————. *Illuminator, Makar, Vates: Visions of Poetry in the Fifteenth Century* (Lincoln, Nebraska 1988).

Edwards, A. S. G., "The Influence and Audience of Lydgate's *Fall of Princes, c.* 1440-1559: A Survey," *Mediaeval Studies* 39 (1977), 424-39.

————. "Lydgate Manuscripts: Some Directions for Future Research," in Pearsall (1983), 15-26.

————. "Lydgate Scholarship: Progress and Prospects," in Yeager (1984), 29-47.

————. and A. W. Jenkins, "A Hymn to the Virgin: By Lydgate?" *Mediaeval Studies* 35 (1973), 60-66.

————. and J. I. Miller, "Stow and Lydgate's 'St. Edmund,'" *NQ* 218 (1973), 365-69.

Farnham, W., *The Medieval Heritage of Elizabethan Tragedy* (Oxford 1936).

Gage, J., "Historical Notices of the Great Bell Tower of the Abbey Church of St. Edmundsbury," *Archaeologia* 23 (1831), 327-33.

————. "Letters from King Henry VI to the Abbot of St. Edmundsbury and to the Alderman and Bailiffs of the Town, for the Suppression of the Lollards," *ibid.* 340.

Galbraith, V. H., "New Documents about Gloucester College," in Salter (1924), 337-86.

Gibson, G., "Bury St. Edmunds, Lydgate, and the *N. Town Cycle*," *Speculum* 56 (1981), 56-90.

Green, R. F., "Three Fifteenth-Century Notes," *ELN* 14 (1976), 14-17 (Note 2 on the date of *The Mumming at Hertford*).

————. "Lydgate and Deguileville Once More," *NQ* 223 (1978), 105-06.

————. *Poets and Princepleasers: Literature and the English Court in the Later Middle Ages* (Toronto 1980).

Griffiths, R. A., *The Reign of King Henry VI: The Exercise of Royal Authority 1422-61* (London 1981).

Hammond, E. P., "Lydgate and the Duchess of Gloucester," *Anglia* 27 (1904), 381-98.

————. "Two British Museum Manuscripts (Harley 2251 and Add. 34360): A Contribution to the Bibliography of John Lydgate," *Anglia* 28 (1905), 1-28.

————. "Ashmole 59 and other Shirley Manuscripts," *Anglia* 30 (1907), 320-48.

————. "Two Tapestry Poems by Lydgate: The *Life of St. George* and the *Falls of Seven Princes*," *Englische Studien* 43 (1910-1911), 10-26.

————. "Lydgate and Coluccio Salutati," *Modern Philology* 25 (1927), 49-57.

————. "Poet and Patron in the *Fall of Princes*: Lydgate and Humphrey of Gloucester," *Anglia* 38 (1914), 121-36.

Hargreaves, H., "Lydgate's 'A Ram's Horn,'" *Chaucer Review* 10 (1976), 255-59.

Harriss, G. L., ed., *Henry V: The Practice of Kingship* (Oxford 1985).

Herbert, J. A., "List of Contents of [BL] MS.14848," in Lord F. Hervey, *The Pinchbeck Register*, 2 vols. (London 1925), 301-54.

Hortis, A., *Studi sulle Opere Latine del Boccaccio* (Trieste 1879), 640-57.

Hyde, I., "Lydgate's 'halff-chongyd latyne': An Illustration," *MLN* 70 (1955), 252-54.

James, M. R., *On the Abbey of S. Edmund at Bury* (*I, The Library; II, The Church*), Octavo Publications of the Cambridge Antiquarian Society, 28 (Cambridge 1895).

————. "Bury St. Edmunds Manuscripts," *English Historical Review* 41 (1926), 251-60.

Kean, P. M., *The Making of English Poetry*, 2 vols. (London 1972), II.210-39.

Keiser, G. R., "*Ordinatio* in the Manuscripts of John Lydgate's *Lyf of Our Lady*: Its Value for the Reader, Its Challenge for the Modern Editor," in *Medieval Literature: Texts and Interpretation*, ed. T. W. Machan, Medieval and Renaissance Texts and Studies, 79 (Binghamton 1991), 139-57.

Kipling, G., "The London Pageants for Margaret of Anjou: A Medieval Script Restored," *Medieval English Theatre* 4 (1982), 5-27.

Knowles, D., *The Religious Orders in England*, Vol. II: *The End of the Middle Ages* (Cambridge 1955), 273-75.

Kuczynski, M. P., *Prophetic Song: The Psalms as Moral Discourse in Late Medieval England* (Philadelphia 1995), 135-48 (Lydgate's Psalm-imitations), 152-64 (*Defence of Holy Church*).

Lampe, D., "Lydgate's Laughter: Lydgate's 'Hors, Sheep and Goose' as Social Laughter," *Annuale Mediaevale* 15 (1974), 150-58.

Lawton, D., "Dullness and the Fifteenth Century," *ELH* 54 (1987), 761-99.

Lawton, L., "The Illustration of Late Medieval Secular Texts, with Special Reference to Lydgate's *Troy Book*," in Pearsall (1983), 41-69.

Lerer, S., *Chaucer and his Readers: Imagining the Author in Late-Medieval England* (Princeton 1993).

Lewis, C. S., *The Allegory of Love* (Oxford 1936), 232-43.

Lowndes, G. A., "History of the Priory at Hatfield Regis, alias Hatfield Broad Oak," *Transactions of the Essex Archaeological Society*, n.s. 2 (1884), 117-52.

MacCracken, H. N., "Additional Light on the *Temple of Glas*," *PMLA* 23 (1908), 128-40.

———. "An English Friend of Charles of Orleans," *PMLA* 26 (1911), 142-80.

———. "King Henry's Triumphal Entry into London, Lydgate's Poem, and Carpenter's Letter," *Archiv* 126 (1911), 75-102.

Machan, T. W., "Textual Authority and the Works of Hoccleve, Lydgate, and Henryson," *Viator* 23 (1992), 281-97.

McFarlane, K. B., *Lancastrian Kings and Lollard Knights* (Oxford 1972).

McKenna, J. W., "Henry VI of England and the Dual Monarchy: Aspects of Royal Political Propaganda, 1422-1432," *Journal of the Warburg and Courtauld Institutes* 28 (1965), 145-62.

McNiven, P., *Heresy and Politics in the Reign of Henry IV: The Burning of John Badby* (Woodbridge 1987).

Miller, J. I., "Lydgate the Hagiographer as Literary Artist," in *The Learned and the Lewed*, ed. L. D. Benson, Harvard Studies in English 5 (Cambridge, MA, 1974), 279-80.

Mooney, L. R., "Lydgate's 'Kings of England' and Another Verse Chronicle of the Kings," *Viator* 20 (1989), 255-89.

Moore, S., "Patrons of Letters in Norfolk and Suffolk *c*. 1450," *PMLA* 27 (1912), 188-207; 28 (1913), 79-105.

Nicolas, Sir H., *Proceedings and Ordinances of the Privy Council of England 1386-1461*, 6 vols. (London 1834-37).

Norton-Smith, J., "Lydgate's Changes in the *Temple of Glas*," *Medium Aevum* 27 (1958), 166-72.

———. "Lydgate's Metaphors," *English Studies* 42 (1961), 90-93.

Ord, C., "Account of the Entertainment of King Henry the Sixth at the Abbey of Bury St. Edmund's," *Archaeologia* 15 (1806), 65-71.

Osberg, R., "The Jesse Tree in the 1432 London Entry of Henry VI: Messianic Kingship and the Rule of Justice," *Journal of Medieval and Renaissance Studies* 16 (1986), 213-32.

Pantin, W. A., *Documents Illustrating the Activities of the General and Provincial Chapters of the English Black Monks 1215-1540*, 3 vols., Camden Society, 3rd series 45, 47, 54 (London 1931-37).

Parr, J., "Astronomical Dating for some of Lydgate's Poems," *PMLA* 67 (1952), 251-58.

———. "The Astronomical Date of Lydgate's *Life of Our Lady*," *Philological Quarterly* 50 (1971), 120-25.

Parry, P. H., "On the Continuity of English Court Pageantry: A Study of John Lydgate and the Tudor Pageant," *Forum for Modern Language Studies* 15 (1979), 222-36.

Patterson, L., "Making Identities in Fifteenth-Century England: Henry V and John Lydgate," in *New Historical Literary Study: Essays on Reproducing Texts, Representing History*, ed. J. N. Cox and L. J. Reynolds (Princeton 1993), 69-107.

Pearsall, D., "The English Chaucerians," in *Chaucer and Chaucerians*, ed. D. Brewer (London 1966), 201-39.

———. *John Lydgate* (London 1970).

———, ed., *Manuscripts and Readers in Fifteenth-Century England: The Literary Implications of Manuscript Study* (Woodbridge 1983).

———. "Signs of Life in Lydgate's *Danse Macabre*," in *Zeit, Tod und Ewigkeit in der Renaissance Literatur*, ed. J. Hogg, Band 3, Analecta Cartusiana 117 (Salzburg 1987), 58-71.

———. "Chaucer and Lydgate," in *Chaucer Traditions: Studies in Honour of Derek Brewer*, ed. R. Morse and B. Windeatt (Cambridge 1990), 39-53.

———. "Lydgate as Innovator," *MLQ* 53 (1992), 5-22.

Renoir, A., *The Poetry of John Lydgate* (London 1967).

Robinson, F. N., "On Two Manuscripts of Lydgate's *Guy of Warwick*," *Harvard Studies and Notes in Philology and Literature* 5 (1899), 177-213.

Rowe, B. J. H., "King Henry VI's Claim to France in Picture and Poem," *Library*, 4th series 13 (1932-33), 77-88.

Ruud, M. B., *Thomas Chaucer*, Research Publications of the University of Minnesota, Studies in Language and Literature, No. 9 (Minneapolis 1926).

Rymer, T., *Foedera*, 20 vols. (London 1727-35).

Salter, H. E., ed., *Snappe's Formulary and Other Records*, Oxford Historical Society, Vol. 80 (Oxford 1924).

Scattergood, V. J., *Politics and Poetry in the Fifteenth Century* (London 1971).

Schirmer, W. F., *John Lydgate: A Study in the Culture of the XVth Century*, tr. A. E. Keep (London 1961; first publ. in German 1952).

Scott, K., "Lydgate's *Lives of Saints Edmund and Fremund*: A Newly-Located Manuscript in Arundel Castle," *Viator* 13 (1982), 335-66.

―――. "*Caveat Lector*: Ownership and Standardization in the Illustration of Fifteenth-Century English Manuscripts," *English Manuscript Studies 1100-1700* 1 (1989), 19-63.

Seymour, M. C., "Some Lydgate Manuscripts: *Lives of SS. Edmund and Fremund* and *Danse Macabre*," *Edinburgh Bibliographical Society Transactions* 5, part 4 (1983-1985), 10-24.

Spearing, A. C., *Medieval Dream Poetry* (Cambridge 1976), 171-76 (on *The Temple of Glass*).

―――. "Lydgate's Canterbury Tale: *The Siege of Thebes* and Fifteenth-Century Chaucerianism," in Yeager (1984), 333-64.

Stow, John, *A Survey of London*, ed. G. L. Kingsford, 2 vols. (Oxford 1908).

Tanner, Thomas, *Bibliotheca Britannico-Hibernica* (London 1748).

Thomson, R. M., *The Archives of the Abbey of Bury St. Edmunds*, Suffolk Records Society, Vol. 21 (Woodbridge 1980).

Torti, A., "From 'History' to 'Tragedy': The Story of Troilus and Criseyde in Lydgate's *Troy Book* and Henryson's *Testament of Cresseid*," in *The European Tragedy of Troilus*, ed. P. Boitani (Oxford 1989), 171-97.

―――. *The Glass of Form: Mirroring Structures from Chaucer to Skelton* (Cambridge 1991), 67-86 (on *The Temple of Glass*).

Trapp, J. B., "Verses by Lydgate at Long Melford," *Review of English Studies*, n.s. 6 (1955), 1-11.

Walls, K., "Did Lydgate Translate the 'Pelerinage de la Vie Humaine'?" *NQ* 222 (1977), 103-05.

Watson, N., "Outdoing Chaucer: Lydgate's *Troy-Book* and Henryson's *Testament of Cresseid* as Competitive Imitations of *Troilus and Criseyde*," in *Shifts and Transpositions in Medieval Narrative: A Festschrift for Dr Elspeth Kennedy*, ed. K. Pratt (Cambridge 1994), 89-108.

Weiss, R., *Humanism in England during the Fifteenth Century*, 3rd edn. (Oxford 1957).

Wickham, G., *Early English Stages 1300-1600*, 2 vols. (London 1959, 1981), I.191-207.

Wilson, J., "Poet and Patron in Early Fifteenth-Century England: John Lydgate's *Temple of Glas*," *Parergon* 11 (1975), 25-32.

Withington, R., *English Pageantry: An Historical Outline* (Cambridge, MA, 1918).

Woolf, R., *The English Religious Lyric in the Middle Ages* (Oxford 1968).

Yeager, R. F., ed., *Fifteenth-Century Studies: Recent Essays* (Hamden, CT, 1984).

1975 1 *Samuel Johnson's Library: An Annotated Guide*, Donald Greene

2 *The Sale Catalogue of Samuel Johnson's Library: A Facsimile Edition*, J. D. Fleeman

3 *Swift's Vision of Evil: A Comparative Study of "A Tale of a Tub" and "Gulliver's Travels,"* vol. 1, *A Tale of a Tub*, Philip Pinkus

4 *Swift's Vision of Evil*, vol. 2, *Gulliver's Travels*, Philip Pinkus

1976 5 *Dryden and Future Shock*, William Frost

6 *Henry Fielding's "Tom Jones" and the Romance Tradition*, Henry K. Miller.

7 *The Achievement of Thomas More*, Richard J. Schoeck

1977 8 *The Postromantic Consciousness of Ezra Pound*, George Bornstein

9 *Eighteenth-Century Arguments for Immortality and Johnson's "Rasselas,"* R. G. Walker

10 *E. M. Forster's Posthumous Fiction*, Norman Page

1978 11 *Paradise in the Age of Milton*, U. Milo Kaufmann

12 *The Slandered Woman in Shakespeare*, Joyce H. Sexton

13 *Jane Austen on Love*, Juliet McMaster

14 *C. S. Lewis's "Great War" with Owen Barfield*, Lionel Adey

1979 15 *The Arnoldian Principle of Flexibility*, William Robbins

16 *Frankenstein's Creation: The Book, The Monster, and Human Reality*, David Ketterer

17 *Christopher Smart's Verse Translation of Horace's "Odes,"* Arthur Sherbo, ed.

18 *Gertrude Stein: Autobiography and the Problem of Narration*, Shirley Neuman

1980 19 *Daniel Defoe's Moral and Rhetorical Ideas*, Robert James Merrett

20 *Studies in Robertson Davies' Deptford Trilogy*, R. G. Lawrence and S. L. Macey, eds.

21 *Pater and His Early Critics*, Franklin E. Court

1981 22 *The Curve of Return: D. H. Lawrence's Travel Books*, Del Ivan Janik

23 *The Educational World of Daniel Defoe*, Donald P. Leinster-Mackay

24 *The Libraries of George Eliot and George Henry Lewes*, William Baker

1982 25 *John Ruskin and Alfred Hunt: New Letters and the Record of a Friendship*, R. Secor

26 *The Cover of the Mask: The Autobiographers in Charlotte Brontë's Fiction*, A. Tromley

27 *Charles Olson and Edward Dahlberg: A Portrait of a Friendship*, John Cech

1983 28 *The Road From Horton: Looking Backwards in "Lycidas,"* J. Martin Evans

29 *Dryden's Dualities*, Ruth Salvaggio

30 *The Return of the Good Soldier: Ford Madox Ford and Violet Hunt's 1917 Diary*, Robert Secor and Marie Secor

ENGLISH LITERARY STUDIES publishes peer-reviewed monographs (usual length, 45,000-60,000 words) on the literatures written in English. The Series is open to a wide range of scholarly and critical methodologies, and it considers for publication bibliographies, scholarly editions, and historical and critical studies of significant authors, texts, and issues. ELS publishes two to five monographs annually.

DATE DUE
